FINDING YOUR VOICE IN RELATIONSHIPS

Stop Managing Your Relationships on Men's Terms

FINDING YOUR VOICE IN RELATIONSHIPS

Stop Managing Your Relationships on Men's Terms

Dr. Ann Davis

ISBN: 978-0-692880-62-3

Contents

Introduction

God, family and myriad relationships have always been my greatest teachers, joys, sorrows, lessons, and inspirations. They've taught me more because of their love, mistreatment, acceptance, and encouragement. Loving and learning in relationship with everyone has helped me to become who I truly am today. This book is dedicated to all those who have come, stayed, will come, and have gone out of my life. Throughout life so far, I have been blessed and am grateful for them all. I look forward to the rest of this superb journey.

Chapter One

———————————————

Far from the North to the South

Early Days – New England Roots

Finding my voice in relationships begins in New England and is a process that continues still. I was born Ann Davis, in Springfield, Massachusetts, the 12th generation, first daughter of New England parents, grandparents, and ancestors, a White Anglo-Saxon Protestant (WASP), the first 12th generation daughter of the General Society of Mayflower Descendants (GSMD) and Daughters of the American Revolution (DAR). Because of that, it took me much of my lifetime to feel comfortable in my skin.

I guess growing up mainly in the Southwest far from the Northeast contributed to feeling that way.

I always felt a little outside that box, yet today, I relish sharing it with my children and grandchildren so they might share it for generations to come with all the integrated parts of that whole as it expands.

Playing outside, asparagus, insects, fireflies, apples, grapes, berries, and making pies are some of my fondest, earliest memories of childhood. I was the apple of my daddy's eye and his first, baby girl. My parents were childhood classmates and friends all through school who had grown up in the same small town where we lived in Palmer, Massachusetts. I came home from the hospital to my Nanalou's home at 32 Thorndike Street where my mom was raised.

Jessica Louise, my mom's mother, was always NanaLou to me; she wanted to be Nana since everyone knew her as Louise, so she was NanaLou. She was an educated, adventurous woman who or whom I never knew well. I must have inherited some of my adventurous spirit and yearning to see the world, though, from her.

I learned when I was much older that she had two college degrees, one from the University of North Dakota where she grew up, then one later from Boston University, both before women got the right to vote – thanks to her father, my great grandfather, and her husband, my mother's father! Wow! That was something back then; they must have been nice men.

NanaLou was a widow at 53 years young. Frances, my mother, was 13 years old when her father died. Mary, my mother's only older sister, died at 10 years old of strep throat before penicillin was invented; my mom was only eight. I can't even imagine how awful that was. It was just Nanalou's family and other relatives of her husband, my grandfather, as he had several brothers. NanaLou had a large home, and there was plenty of room for us all.

From what I was told years later, NanaLou wasn't happy about my mother marrying my dad. I guess that is why living in her home didn't last very long. We moved onto my dad's parents' property before I was two. My dad took their barn down and built our little home, where my earliest memories of so many wonderful things all happened.

Childhood Joys

I loved chasing squirrels, swinging in the big apple tree, fingers glowing from squished fireflies, and bringing my Grammie mason jars of bugs off the asparagus plants in her garden and making berry pies with her. I learned about wasps, how to read and write, listened to the Red Sox that were always on my grandpa Dave's radio, and how to string buttons. All the necessary, enjoyable, tasty, homemade things have lasted and served me well.

My dad's parents' barn that became our house I vaguely remember. It was a little, two-story house my dad had built set back from the street quite a distance and beside his parents' home. It was just the right size for my parents, me and soon to be my brother or sister, as they didn't know yet back then. I was very young and lived in it for only a few years, but oh what a few years they were. I remember going up and down the stairs, and I can see the kitchen cabinets and front porch and yard. We moved into it before my brother, Davey, was born. He was one of my second birthday presents.

I don't think he was my favorite present much of the time at first. When Davey arrived, he got all the attention; I wanted to drink a bottle again and wet my pants. I don't think all that worked for me too long. I really did love Davey to pieces, though! I know I was too young to remember, but it's from stories my grandparents and parents told me later that I can recall; those were great times with my folks, Grammie and Grandpa, and Davey until we moved from our hometown in Palmer.

A Special Birthday Present

Davey and I were born the same exact day two years apart, March 3, Pisces – the two fish. We celebrated most of our early birthdays together. Davey had a chocolate cake, and I had an angel food cake. That is what we liked, so mom made us each our own. We got to sit at opposite ends of the table and blow out our candles.

What a treat always! I loved my angel food cake and Davey loved his chocolate cake. I don't remember if we tried each other's cake, as angel food has always been my favorite. I'm not much of a cake or pie person really, but cookies – oh yay!

Mom cooked almost everything from scratch, because that is the way dad liked it. Mom like my Grammie, too, made lots of other things herself such as: bread, rolls, hot dog and hamburger buns, cakes, pies, cookies, snicker doodles, date bars, and another favorite of mine: her delicious cream puffs with custard inside.

Those were almost as grand as my angel food cake. My mother was a very talented homemaker. My mother was terrific; she taught my younger sister, Susie, and me so many skills and much growing up as we got older. But I am getting ahead of myself; Susie wasn't with us yet.

My father attended William and Mary University in Virginia after high school and wanted to be a medical doctor. More than likely since his dad had heart trouble and couldn't work once he was middle aged, dad left university much to his mother's dismay to help them out right before the U.S. entered WWII and off he went.

My mother after high school attended Pine Manor, which began as part of Wellesley College, for two years in Massachusetts, close to home, then she trekked off to Santa Monica, California to UCLA to study fine art. When she graduated, both she and NanaLou returned to New England, where my mother got a job as a commercial artist for a few years at Remington Corporation before she married my dad after WWII ended and he came home.

Time with Grammie & Grandpa

I must have spent a lot of time at my grand-parents' house once Davey arrived, as I remember being with Grammie a lot. Grammie smelled like April violets, and loved me to pieces. She was always busy cooking, hanging clothes, and taking care of my Grandpa and the house.

Grandpa's heart wasn't well, and he took naps a lot, even though he wasn't very old. I had the seeds planted early of good health and an education to cherish later.

Grammie let me do things with her like help hold the clothespins and hand them to her while she hung the clothes out. The clothesline was right on the back porch; I can still see it in my mind's eye. It was a wheel with a cord around it that you pinned the clothes to on one side, then pulled the cord and out they went into the air to dry.

They must have been attached somewhere at the other end but I don't remember what that looked like because I was always on the back porch helping and watching the clothes leave. I do remember the big mud dabber wasp nest, though, and how one or two were always flying around and in and out of it. Grammie always told me not to bother them, and they wouldn't bother me. Grammie was great at reassuring me, as well as teaching me what they were good for and did.

Whenever she would make a pie for my grandpa, I would get to make my size pies, pick the berries off the bushes in the yard to put in my pie, and Grammie would give me some of the pie dough from the big pies she made to use for mine, and I would roll it out and fill my little pan. When I was done, she would bake mine with hers in the oven. It was so much FUN!

When the clothes we'd hung out were dry and ready to be put away, Grammie would take me upstairs with her. I would get to sit on the floor in the bedroom, and she would get her button tin (an old tin coffee can; I have that very same one today - Austin, Nichols, & Co., Inc. New York "cup value our first consideration") and lay out newspapers for me to empty out the buttons onto; then I could sort through all the different buttons and string together whichever little buttons I chose.

She had taught me how to string them all together with a sewing needle and I loved to do this. Doing this was one of my favorite things to do at her house. I bet it kept me busy for quite some time while she finished up a chore or two. I thought it was great and treasure that coffee tin that is full of pretty mother of pearl and other antique buttons still today.

I loved playing in the yard – it was big. I could run and do so much. There was a swing in the big apple tree between the houses, a birdbath, and lots of squirrels I could chase. Grammie always warned me not to try to catch them because they might bite and hurt me. My grandparents had tons of concord and red grapes all around the side porch that tasted yummy, and there was so much to intrigue me outside.

Once Davey got older he loved it too; it was a big yard setback from the street with my grandparents' house on one side closer to Maple Street and their garden behind their house that ran the whole distance back behind our house too, so we got to play outside in the yard and garden often – chasing birds and squirrels, swinging and eating grapes, and just having fun being kids. Davey was fun to hang out and do things with when he got a little bigger. He'd pick bugs with me off our grandparents' asparagus patch. We'd fill jars Grammie would give us.

Sometimes mom and us would go picking blueberries too – boy were they yummy. We'd take buckets and pick them just out in the hills – I don't know exactly where, but it is something I'll never forget. They are one of my favorites, and remind me of home when I was little. I still love them today!

A Strong Spiritual Foundation

Davey and I were raised in St. Paul's Unitarian Universalist, a big old Granite stone church down the street that our parents took us to from our very beginnings. I'm not sure both my grandparents went with us since my grandpa was ill. But I bet they did, as I know my dad was raised in that church, attended and served with my grandparents even when he had grown up.

I was fortunate to have Christian parents who made sure I knew God and had a faith to call on when life throws you curves and/or the valleys seem to outweigh the peaks at times traveling along life's highway on our own. As the journey winds and weaves and things don't always turn out the way we had thought and prayed they would, my faith has remained a strength and comfort that I relish. It has carried me through my life's trials and tribulations as well as its many great adventures. To know that my Heavenly Father and His love are always with me is a solace for God is always with us.

As we grew up, I always remember going to church and I enjoyed the Bible stories, learning and getting to know them well. I was curious about all religions and wanted to experience many; my dad encouraged me to do so. I remember going with friends to a variety of churches that were different from my own home church.

But as a teenager, I didn't much like church services much because I found most of the sermons boring, and I wanted to sleep in on Sunday mornings. Also as a teenager, it took a special pastor to reach me and what was going on in my mind, life, and the world. But it was a requirement in our home to go to Sunday school and church on Sundays. I am thankful that it was now, as my faith has sustained me and always will. I truly believe in a higher power and the mysteries of life that science and man are not able to answer well that add truth to the mysteries of our existence, world, and universe.

Short Southern Stay - Elizabethtown, Kentucky

We traveled 955 miles southwest to Elizabethtown, Kentucky before I was four years old because my dad was stationed at Fort Knox. My parents rented a house in Elizabethtown that was only a 16-mile drive north for my dad to Fort Knox and his work. We weren't there too long; I don't remember much other than what my mother told me years later when I asked who the old lady was that came to have cookies and coffee with her. She explained she owned the house we rented for the short time my daddy was stationed there.

I don't remember her name but she didn't have all her teeth so she seemed older to me, though she wasn't old, and younger than my mom, who was 30 then. She had grown up on a large farm that was hard work. By summer we were going home again to our house next to Grammie and Grandpa's.

Back to New England to Start School

Grandpa Dave was a loving grandpa; I remember him riding in my wagon and playing with me outside in the yard sometimes although not too often.

Grandpa was the one who spent a part of each day teaching me how to read and write for primary school before I was four. He would read books to me, show me how to sound out all the letters, and explain all the pictures, colors and elaborate on them for me so that I would know how to read and write some before I went to school.

Grandpa Dave would sit in his big, old armchair that he loved and kick one leg across the arm of it, so I could climb up and sit between his legs to look at all the words and pictures in the books. I don't know where all the books came from – maybe they were my dad's when he was a boy, and I don't remember many of the stories, but I loved to sit with him, read and learn.

It was my dad's chair after grandpa passed away, and when I lost my dad I inherited that same antique armchair that I now have in my office. It has had many lives and been recovered many times, but the memories it holds are still near and dear to my heart. It's a comfort to me and reminds family and me of them both, as if they are sometimes here with me – like as I write this book and work.

We are all connected after all – just six degrees of separation and maybe even less like three degrees

I heard recently, right? It's a very small world from space for sure our view of the Earth "blue marble" we inhabit.

I started school at four and a half years old in first grade at Park Street School. They didn't have a kindergarten in the school at that time. I loved to walk to school each day and home with my mother or Grammie, as it wasn't very far from our house. I loved school. It was a two-story brick building with large windows. I had the same teacher my parents had in first grade.

I don't remember her name or much about her. I had to raise my hand in class to go to the bathroom and probably waited too long once to do so. But she didn't call on me in time, and I wet myself. I was so upset. I cried and my Grammie had to come get me. It must have been later in the year.

When so young and often throughout our life, we remember the awkward moments more so than the enjoyable ones. We all need to strive to create more heartwarming and gratifying moments for everyone.

Moving South – North Carolina Bound

Shortly after I started school, my father got transferred to Camp Lejeune, North Carolina with the Marine Corps. Davey was two years old and not in school, so I stayed with my grandparents to finish out the school year. This was fine with me and fun too!

Grammie and Grandpa continued to love and teach me lots, and I enjoyed my time with them. I sent my mom, dad, and Davey letters about what I did and stuff I made in school. I was given some of those letters many years later when an adult by my mother as she had saved them for me.

I don't remember if my mother knew yet when they left for Camp Lejeune or told me she was pregnant with my little sister, Sue, born the first part of June. I met her that summer when my parents and siblings picked me up to take me back with them to our new home. After we all visited, we said our goodbyes to my grandparents. I was going south with my family now to our new house in North Carolina.

When you are just five years old, safe and loved, always with family in the same place, life is rooted, secure, and has a solid foundation from which to grow and flourish when experiencing new adventures!

Moving to a new place meant so many new differences. I was home with my folks, Davey, and now I had a new, baby sister, Sue. WOW! We had a big house with a playground right beside it and a movie theater next door, too. Mommy needed extra help with the three of us now, as we were close in age and a handful with Susie being brand new too. My dad hired Minniebelle to help my mother during the week with us and the chores too.

From what my mother told me, I was somewhat distant toward Minniebelle, as I imagine I would have been with anyone I didn't know at first. But that ended quickly, and I took to Minniebelle like a duck to water. I grew to know and love her as she loved me and cared for us all. I got to go with my dad in his MG to take her home after work. What a joy that was for me as the oldest. It was something I looked forward to in the afternoon each day. The visual memories in my mind make grand impressions.

Marine Corps Base Camp Lejeune didn't look anything like Palmer. For one thing, it was a military base, so all kinds of military equipment and personnel were everywhere – soldiers, boats, helicopters, tanks, and jeeps, which was different. The weather was different too and there were hurricanes!

I still remember the wind blew so hard the telephone poles leaned sideways toward the ground like they were going to pop off their wires. Looking out our windows, the rain looked like curtains of water. It was scary; I'm glad Minniebelle and my mom were there, so I didn't get too frightened.

I attended a new school when I started second grade that year. It was in a bungalow-type building off the ground with steps up to it. I didn't like it as much, though, as Park Street school in first grade, and had bad dreams about that school in N. Carolina for a long time even after we moved west. I don't remember why. Something bothered me, though. Years later, I met and made several friends in Fallbrook who had also lived at Camp Lejeune the same year I did and one of the ladies said she had felt the same way.

We all ended up in the San Diego area after our military fathers were transferred. We were off soon enough, though, before I finished second grade. Dad got transferred to Southern California, so far from my little hometown in Massachusetts.

But life has a way of directing you, and as Dr. Seuss wrote, *Oh, The Places You'll Go!* (Geisel, 1988).

The Marine Corps Base Camp Pendleton, the Corps' largest West Coast expeditionary training facility north of San Diego, was where my father was off to as he was being sent to Korea. I vaguely remember the Marine base although I see it now often driving from San Diego to Los Angeles.

We all left North Carolina almost as soon as my youngest brother, Ned, was born. He was only two months old when we moved into our new home in Crown Point on Mission Bay. It was just my mother and the four of us. Now she really had her hands full and no help from Minniebelle and my dad off in the Korean War.

But what a paradise it turned out to be for my mom and the four of us. Our next-door neighbor, Frances, a registered nurse, had two girls, Marie and Amy, the same age as me and Susie. Altogether there were 52 kids on our block; Davey met lots of boys his age to play with too. We all became fast friends, and everyone knew everyone else. We played outside together and had loads of fun in the sun; there were no snowstorms or hurricanes here.

San Diego was booming! We all loved California; especially my mom, because the weather made it easier rather than having four seasons like in the Northeast. San Diego would remain home for many years to come.

Chapter Two

_____

Becoming Yourself

San Diego, California – SoCal

Once we were settled, I was back in school to finish second grade. What a difference between the Northeast and Southwest or even the Southeast!

I was no foreigner to new things and places. Crown Point Elementary was a big school with a large playground. Here I was far from the small town back east where I was born. We lived on a street with lots of other kids, and I made friends and played with them after school sometimes. Mostly, though, I played with Davey and Susie around the house and in our backyard until I was older; our backyard was spacious and filled with fruit trees.

Since Crown Point is a peninsula, we lived close to the bay surrounding it, and my mother put us in swim lessons so we could learn how to swim during the school vacations and summers. We all became strong swimmers. I started dance classes too: ballet, tap, and jazz to begin with and they would increase to include acrobatics, Spanish, ballroom, and hula as the years passed.

I loved dance and dreamt of being a dancer one day. Soon, summer ended, school started and ended, summer began, school started again, and my daddy came home.

Road Trip on Route 66

The summer I was seven, our whole family drove back east for a visit. I remember it was so far, and I saw so many new and different things. We drove past the Indian reservations; the Indian ladies were selling jewelry and other things alongside the road. They looked so pretty with ribbons in their hair and their traditional dress was so colorful.

We visited Mesa Verde National Park, and I got to go into the ancient, Pueblo Indian cliff dwellings with my dad.

Further east were mountains and big cities. It was great to see my grandparents and NanaLou. We had a great visit, and on the way back home we stopped to see Nanalou's siblings, my mother's uncle, aunt, and cousin in Minneapolis.

Uncle Walter was a medical doctor, and he gave me a jar of hard sour ball candies that were all different colors. He was very tall. Aunt Mamie was not well and bedridden, so Cousin Mable took care of her. They had both lived in Santa Monica when my mother visited in her teens with NanaLou after her husband, my grandpa I never knew, passed away. Having visited California when she was young was a contributing factor for my mother going to UCLA later.

We also stopped in Yellowstone National Park on the way home and saw the geysers and animals. What a memorable trip, and at seven years old I remembered it and can still see so many of those places we traveled to and family members I saw again and met for the very first time in my mind's eye today. It was grand!

I didn't know at seven years old that it would be many years before I saw NanaLou again and several before Grammie, too. I was so blessed to have had my grandparents and NanaLou and their extended family members close for those first five years as caregivers to teach me so much when I was young along with my parents. I had a great, safe and secure, well-rooted childhood upbringing that was a blessing, and I am thankful.

Traveling with family to several other places when I was so young exposed me to diverse people, places, foods, and events that broadened my world, and those memories remained and influenced my future paths and experiences along with the stories I heard from my parents about travels they had taken themselves and with my grandparents as well as other trips their family members took.

Back Home for School Again

The rest of elementary school seemed to pass quickly as I got acclimated and met friends. Davey started and we'd walk together in the morning once he entered first grade. I enjoyed the monkey bars and recess as well as lunch in the cafeteria.

Kate was one of my best friends. Her mother worked in the cafeteria. I remember the food being good and we also had ice cream bars and big homemade cookies we could buy for a nickel. I liked the peanut butter and oatmeal raisin cookies.

Nowadays, things are different and no one can have peanuts in schools. We had art, music, and plays even in elementary school. I remember the cafeteria being the auditorium and being in and seeing performances. Our schools were all open without bars, gates, and fences and lots of windows for daydreaming and wondering about the universe.

I also remember getting shots – yuck! I always fainted. I still have an aversion to them and hospitals are trying for me. Having those you love most so ill when you are real young, hearing about those you love losing family members as you get a little older, then knowing others that die suddenly or are ill and recognizing issues that might be genetic and affect more of those you love can influence your feelings, future choices and vocation.

I guess that is why I love nutrition, healthy lifestyle choices, wellness and preventive medicine so. My father always told us he'd rather pay for wholesome food than doctor and hospital bills. A dear colleague and friend of mine told me something her father always said, you dig your grave with your teeth. It's true!

I was lucky to be able to go to dance class and learn so many different dances. I loved to dance, and my mom let me take other classes like Pointe,

Tahitian, and I continued ballroom, Spanish, Hula, jazz, tap, and acrobatics too.

We got to do shows at the Del Mar Fairgrounds and parades in different towns. I practiced at home, and when Davey and Susie were older they took dance classes, too. Susie and I would do acrobatics together and practice with our friends, Marie and Amy, who lived next door.

We all learned to swim well too after all our summer lessons. Growing up on our block with so many other kids was fun because we all went to the same school and got to play outside after school until dinner. We'd all play games like Hide and Seek, Hopscotch, Marbles, Red Rover, Red light, Green light; Mother may I, Simon says and others. It was entertaining!

When I was in sixth grade, my teacher, Mrs. Sims, taught us how to do ceramics. I liked learning how to do ceramics and making things a lot. We got to make gifts by pouring liquid clay into molds. I have the little boy Christmas caroler I gave my parents. The clay was fun and art became something I enjoyed. I had seen my mother do art at home. She worked as a commercial artist back east before she married my dad. She completed college and graduated from the University of California, Los Angeles, majoring in Fine Art after attending Wellesley in Massachusetts for two years.

She could draw and paint pictures, and would do projects for the PTA, Girl Scouts and Cub Scouts, our church and as a volunteer. She taught Susie and me how to do chores, take care of a house, set a table, wash dishes, and such.

Most of the time, we didn't want to do chores, but taking turns made it easier and getting an allowance was a great incentive. Mom also taught us to sew, crochet, knit, cook, and bake, as we got a little older. She was so talented and creative, and got to stay at home and take care of us all when we were young – not easy or just one job though it takes a myriad of talents.

Most of my friends' mothers stayed home and were homemakers. It was nice because we went to their houses after school and had our friends over, too. All the things you learn, experience, see, enjoy, and do when you're young develop the talents you have that expand as you grow up and mature. Studies show that people who have satisfying relationships with family, friends, and their community are happier, have fewer health problems, and live longer.

The Complex Teen Years

Next year, I would be off to seventh grade and junior high school, as it was called back then; now it's middle school. It was farther from my house in Crown Point and two stories, with an auditorium for all sorts of school elections, meetings, and talent shows. It had a gymnasium for physical education class and sports. We also had music, art, and shop classes: metal, wood, and home economics, too. I got to walk to school and home. The Frosty Shop was close to the school, and we would stop after school for ice cream and to visit with our friends.

I enjoyed school, but there were a lot more students from several elementary schools in the area, so I didn't know as many people. All the classes were separate, so you weren't with the friends you knew all the time or in the same class. I didn't get in trouble, or have difficulty with my studies, in fact I was bored most of the time.

However, I was only 11 years old when I started seventh grade and younger than many of the other students, as I started first grade earlier back east. I remember my parents telling me later the school wanted to move me ahead a year, but they said no because socially I would have been so young throughout high school. As it was, I turned 17, rather than 16, right before graduation.

The social activities at school didn't seem to me to work so well. I knew plenty of girls and boys, and we all run around together, but I didn't have a boyfriend (not that I needed one, but if all your friends have one, you wonder at that age what's wrong with you).

I was also a year younger than most of my friends in the same grade since I had started first grade back east when I was four years old.

My parents were strict, and I had dance classes, recitals, and outside school activities that I enjoyed, so I didn't join clubs in school or do sports outside of our school physical education class.

I loved sports and played tennis, softball, and volleyball in school. We also learned different dances in PE. The boys' gym classes would join the girls' classes, so we'd have partners to dance with and learn how to square dance and waltz. Since I already loved to dance, I thought that was terrific!

This was also a hard time for me; I guess it is for most teens, to this day, no matter who they are. I had a lot of good girlfriends and knew a lot of classmates. It seemed that a lot of girls had steady boyfriends, were members of the clubs, and got to attend all the events at school or even outside school.

Still, though I knew the boys and girls too, I didn't have a boyfriend or belong to many clubs. I guess I was doing other things, like dance class and such. There were dances for only a dollar admission at the Pacific Beach Recreation Center on the weekends with live bands. They were great bands, too; you'd call them boy bands today and they were then.

Although I went, I don't remember getting to dance much. We'd all go to the movies at the Roxy Theater on Friday nights, but my girlfriends usually went to meet the boys they liked.

I remember one Friday my dad dropped three of us off. The two girls I was with were not going into the movies, even though I did because the boy I liked worked in the theater so I could see him. I don't think he knew I liked him, though. My girlfriends went to meet their boyfriends, who were older. My dad must have turned around and seen them walking down the street, so he came to check to make sure I was in the theater. Later, he called their parents to let them know what they'd done. I wasn't included in other activities much after that because they didn't want to get in trouble.

I remember I slept over at a friend's house and we all slept in the backyard. They didn't clue me in as to their plans; they waited until I fell asleep and snuck out of the yard to visit their boyfriends across the street in the same neighborhood.

I woke up to them coming back into the yard much later. It made me feel like I didn't fit in or there was something wrong with me. Most of my friends had more freedom than I did or their parents weren't as suspicious as to what they might do if no one checked on them. My dad was strict and checked on me to make sure I was where I said I was going and doing what I said I was doing.

At 12 years old, I felt like no one liked me. It made junior high school tough.

When I was in eighth grade, Grammie came to San Diego to live with us. I loved having her here, and she spoiled me with attention, like when I was little and lived with her.

She'd brush my hair for hours in the evening, and we'd talk about all kinds of things. She wasn't very taken with California, as she had grown up and lived on the East Coast all her life. She thought

California was too relaxed, and it is quite different compared to New England. Grammie was more comfortable back east.

My best friend at the time, Kate, was upset about the way things were at home because her father drank so much, probably because he was a painter and lead was still used in the paint. We now know that it's toxic and can make one quite sick.

She asked me to run away with her one afternoon after school and since I thought everyone disliked me I said okay. Off we walked after school. Running away we passed a classmate, Guy, outside his house and stopped to chat. He gave us an apple and candy bar.

Kate and I split those, as they were all we had to eat that evening. We didn't get very far walking along the road before the police stopped us, as it was getting dark. As the patrol car pulled over and the officer asked what we were doing and where we were going, I immediately said we're running away from home. I guess I was naïve; I didn't think fast enough on my feet. Our running away ended safely; thank GOD!

The police officers already had two young men in their car, so they put us in the front seat and one policeman rode in back with the boys. They dropped the boys off, then took us to the La Jolla substation. Kate's parents picked her up; the police ended up taking me home because my Grammie fainted when she heard I was okay, and it took my parents too long to come get me. That was a horrid experience for me; I felt terrible about it.

Instead of getting quite mad, my father appealed to my appetite. He told me what a good dinner they all had and asked what I had. My dad was such a smart man; I learned this once I was an adult and began to get my life together. Later, once in graduate school and working to achieve my dreams, we talked more about topics that interested us both. Dad always wanted the best for us.

My parents were great friends, respected each other, communicated and worked together and it benefited us all. That experience changed me some, I felt blessed my parents cared as much as they did and ashamed I had caused Grammie such stress. My parents worked hard to keep us all busy in activities we enjoyed that kept us from getting into trouble. I am thankful they had the wherewithal and the energy to do so.

Today, I'm eternally grateful to have had all of them around growing up and that I was taught etiquette, which I believe is as valuable as a great education.

Grammie didn't live with us very long. When she came to stay with us, I didn't know that she was ill. She stayed with us so my dad was with her when she had facial surgery for Tic douloureux or trigeminal neuralgia, which she had suffered with for some time. It is a severe, stabbing pain to one side of the face. It stems from one or more branches of the nerve that supplies sensation to the face, the trigeminal nerve. It is considered one of the most painful conditions to affect people.

She had the surgery in Los Angeles at Cedars Sinai Hospital with a neurosurgeon my father knew. I remember Grammie telling me later when she was recovering at home with us all that she was in the hospital the same time as Lucille Ball. I watched as she healed, and I asked questions. I remember thinking, I don't ever want this terrible disease. She had the nerve that controlled the left side of her face cut, as she had alcohol injections for the pain previously, but those stop working after a while. Surgery to cut the nerve where it affects each section on that side of her face is the last thing doctors did then for the pain.

Grammie looked in a mirror and practiced for a long time to teach her muscles to react so that when she smiled both sides of her mouth went up.

Surgery left her without feeling in the left side of her face. I remember quite a while after she had totally healed she walked too close to a tree branch that brushed her face and scratched it and she didn't feel it. It was better to not suffer the pain but there were other consequences with which she had to cope. This continued to shape my passion for preventative health and wellness as I grew up and was exposed to others' situations.

It's fascinating how the situations and experiences throughout life within all our relationships lead us to what we wish to do in life and how we hope to work to serve others.

Halfway through 9th grade, Grammie went back home. School got more enjoyable, walking home with my girlfriends and going to the ocean with them on the weekends. At 13, my youngest brother, Ned, was six years old, so my mother would let us all go to the bay together. We could all swim well, and Davey was 10 and Susie was eight years old – we were all just about two years apart. I was old enough to watch my siblings when my parents went to the movies or out to dinner with friends.

My dad was out of the Marine Corps now and working different shifts, so if it was night shift, and he was sleeping during the day on weekends, going to the bay kept it quiet in the house for him and nice for us. I also started babysitting for others in junior high since I lived close to resorts like Vacation Village (now Paradise Point) that needed babysitters for guests.

Many movie stars and sports teams visited San Diego, and we were paid well. I babysat some weekends for neighbors who took me with them for the whole weekend to resorts.

I watched their children, who had a nice time, and they enjoyed themselves, too, away from home. It was super and good money then! I remember going to Warner Hot Springs in the mountains north of Santa Ysabel on the way to Palomar Mountain, which was fabulous. Their hot spring pools are so big and nice! I loved sailing, too, as my parents had Davey and I take sabot sailing lessons at the Mission Bay Yacht Club.

Summers and weekends were the best. My parents kept us busy, and we stayed out of trouble and enjoyed growing up for the most part. Junior high (middle school) was probably the most uncomfortable time for me socially, as a young teenager trying to figure myself and everyone else out along with questioning why life seems so complicated.

What you enjoy and don't enjoy, who you are, and where you fit in or want to fit in with all else in your world at that age is paramount. Adolescence, I thought, was hard. Hormones run rampant; one's body is changing so much that healthy nutrition, water, sleep, exercise, and a balanced lifestyle are key to coping with those growing pains.

Again, I'm thankful that my dad knew that good nutrition prevented disease and unnecessary trips to the doctor, and a balanced lifestyle along with plenty of sleep was important. I remember having to go to bed early, but teenage bodies need the most sleep, and he wanted some quiet time in the evening for just he and my mom.

It seems smart now that I am older and a parent myself, and grandparent, but I remember it being hard to go to bed so early and not feeling tired. It kept me healthy and sharp enough to do all the activities we all did, though. How I loved those. Dancing and sailing were the BEST!

It all passes quickly and changes. Soon we were all ninth graders and going to graduate. We ruled the school and thought we knew it all by then. I was still dancing and loving it; I did USO shows, ballroom dancing at the Women's Club, fairs, and parades all over the county and nearby towns.

There was an all school talent show, and I did a jazz dance to Maurice Williams and the Zodiacs' song, *Stay*. When the year ended, we graduated and got all dressed up fancy for our graduation ceremony. Afterwards, Jack, who I had known since elementary school and liked, invited me out. We drove downtown in a limo to the El Cortez Hotel, the tallest building in downtown San Diego back then with the world's first outside glass elevator to have lunch.

It was an amazing day and my first date ever. After all the adjustments to the newness of junior high, those three school years were over and ended on a grand note. Next, we were all off to Mission Bay High school, home of the Buccaneers. I was a teenager for sure now at 14 years old even though most of my classmates were already 15 and some were even 16.

High school was exciting with all its football games, baseball, track, other sports, new classes and driver's education, so we'd all be driving soon. We were sophomores, just like at the beginning of junior high as seventh graders, pea greens (such nicknames – I wonder if they are the same now or even allowed or if seventh, eighth and ninth graders even have nicknames at all other than those indicating their number of years in school).

There were a lot more students in high school much older than me; many drove their own cars to school. That was something to look forward to, but for now I walked each morning around the bay and met my friends to walk with on the way to school. It wasn't far, and I liked it. Mission Bay was different back then, not fancy or dredged, no parking lots or restrooms. The road dropped off, down to a bank, and water came right up to it.

The islands were still there and mudflats at low tide. There was a dirt path along the side of it through the cattails and grasses, it was not crowded, clean, and the water was full of marine life: sea cucumbers, starfish, snails, stingrays, small fish, and other sea life. It was paradise and full of things to discover.

There was a large, older, run-down home at the end of Lamont Street that we all called a haunted house. Who knows if it really was? Looking east of Crown Point the sight was hills, not many homes, and the University of San Diego was smaller then but loomed large.

Stephanie and I were best friends, and her parents were so nice. Her older brother, Randy, went to high school too. Stephanie and I tried out for JV cheerleading and practiced together a lot. It was fun and we liked cheering.

Stephanie was chosen, but I didn't get chosen. I was bummed, and felt bad, but got over it. I joined gymnastics and I water skied with my friend, Kristy, most weekends since San Diego had such great weather all year. I loved water skiing and we'd hang out at the bay all day and go real early in the morning when the water was clear as glass.

Her Uncle Larry had a big ski boat, and she and I and her brothers and uncle's kids all went; there were always a lot of us. I learned to ski well even on one ski. I had a high school friend, Cheryl, who water skied slalom and jump courses; she was a fantastic water skier. Not me; I went to have a good time and have fun learning to ski, jump the wake, keep from falling in the bay, ski on just one ski, take off from the beach, and come into the beach to step out of that ski and walk up on the beach easily – that was plenty tough for this kid. I was glad I got to learn, go so much and have a great time always.

I didn't drive yet, of course, as I was only 14 but could take driver's education the beginning of my junior year and get my driving permit. I did that in fall of 1962 and completed it, then got my permit but only drove sometimes with either my mom or dad.

I was younger than most in my class in high school having started school back east in first grade before I was five. I rode to school, though, with my classmate, Janice, junior year. She was already driving and had a car. Several of us did as Janice lived close and would pick each of us up on her way to school.

We each paid her a dollar a week for gas; that helped her out, and gas was only 25 cents per gallon most of the time. I felt so much more grown up being able to do this instead of walk, but looking back I was still so young. When you are that age you never think so, though. I was so protected and naïve about so much of life. I was looking forward to driving and having a car hopefully of my own.

Spring came soon, and I turned 16 – Yes! Now I could get my driver's license, and I did. I passed! Yippee! My parents let me drive their cars some of the time, so my driving improved steadily. I got to practice around town, and once they knew they could trust me I was able to use their car myself more often. But it was almost summer, and we always hung out at the ocean all day and walked there or swam across the bay from Stephanie's to the Catamaran Hotel that was cool.

What I considered bad news came that July when my parents explained to us all that we were moving to Salina, Kansas. What? It was my senior year with all my friends I'd known since second grade; I didn't want to go and the parents of a couple great girlfriends of mine on the same block said I could live with them for the last year of high school. My parents wouldn't hear of it. I was going to have to move to Kansas – OMG!

My father received a promotion with the job he held at General Dynamics connected to a division of GD at the time called General Atomics that required he take a transfer position for the next two years at the Strategic Air Command (SAC) base there in Salina. Come August, the summer of my junior year, we were moving to the Midwest – ugh – from San Diego, no less at the height of the sixties with surfing, the Beach Boys, and everything that I had known in SoCal for the past 10 years of my life was in vogue.

I would discover, however, at 16, that there was a lot more to our country's people and places that I didn't know at all yet. Kansas with all its differences had a lot of things to offer about the world at that time.

I really saw for the first time much about segregation and inequality that was just coming to the forefront with the Civil Rights Movement of the sixties. For the first time in my recollection, I was an outsider and different from my classmates and not readily accepted since I was from California. I noticed most knew nothing of California except what television was showing them.

This was a skewed picture of what life really is like that so many across the globe get of the U.S. still today. Even when we at home don't have the opportunities to see other places in our world, we don't seem to relish all the freedoms we have in the U.S., along with the abundance of opportunity to do whatever our hearts and souls set out to accomplish.

It is that American dream that sets us apart from the rest. Thanks to all those that sacrifice, protect and serve us all so we might keep those foundational values alive.

The friends I met and got to know first in classes at school were those like me – new, from other places, or different. Denise was from a military family. Her father was stationed in Panama, but her grandmother lived in Salina. Denise had moved to live with her grandmother because she wanted to become a medical doctor and schooling was better here in the states.

She was in my physiology class. I remember competing with her on tests, as I too wanted to be a doctor although not as deeply then as she did. She was very serious about her studies and scored higher than me every time if only by a couple points. I couldn't beat her as I recall.

Denise worked at the hospital in town after school as a volunteer nurse's helper, candy striper, as the position was known then based on the uniform. I also became friends with Othello Meadows.

We were in study hall together, he was on the football team, and his sense of humor was fantastic! He kept me in stitches.

I used to give him rides home after school. Othello lived on the north side of town, and we had moved into a house on the opposite side back then south of Kansas Wesleyan University, where I would go to do my homework in the library after school each day.

I knew when I first drove Othello home after school that all the houses weren't the same. It reminded me of North Carolina and riding with my daddy to take Minniebelle home. Those experiences got across the essence of the Civil Rights Movement for me, as many of my future relationships and experiences would continue to do.

When we first got to Salina in August, I thought I'd die. The weather was so hot and there were so many insects. I used to get up right after sunrise before much of the town was awake and walk up and down the main street and around the neighborhoods to look at everything. It was nice to walk and look around that early because it wasn't too hot yet.

I missed the ocean and my friends. I wrote letters and heard from a few but most were too busy to write and I wasn't there. The whole beach and surfing scene was far away and Kansas was flat with lots of farms and a small town and no water at all close. I missed the music and it was the year the Beatles arrived on the scene with their first album. I had to go the Sears store to get it. I missed California even though I really liked the differences in Salina.

I think Kansas was the first time in my life where other white classmates looked and snickered about me walking in the halls with a black man. It wasn't that classmates weren't mixed or from all over in San Diego at our schools. I hadn't been around classmates until then that made me feel like I was acting in a way that wasn't acceptable to them.

In Salina, there was a distinct black section of town to the north, as well as segregated black churches. Even though the only public high school was integrated at the time due to Brown v. Board of Education 1954, the town was still so distinctly segregated. I loved to dance and sing so I'd listen outside the black churches some Sunday evenings around dusk when service was in session – God was as happy with their praise and rejoicing as I was.

I would just sit in the car out front with the windows rolled down and listen to their praise through song. What a gospel celebration, and it sounded like they enjoyed it so much. I really liked it a lot and didn't have the courage to join them inside. They made the churches I attended when young, with their choir songs, sound so lackluster.

Surprise - my dad's job ended sooner than expected and we were off to California. Dad surprised me my senior year when we got back to San Diego with my first car, a 1940 Ford Coupe Deluxe. This began my love of 1930s-40s hot rods that continues today. He bought it from the elderly lady across the street, Mrs. Jones. It was one of the best cars I've ever had. Today my goal is to have a 32' hot rod, 3-window, metal body Ford Coupe.

What a surprise and great 16th birthday present! I was so jazzed! My dad made me fix the radio and windshield wipers as it had been sitting garaged for a few years. Mrs. Jones was happy to sell it to him for me, and he paid her $500, a lot back then and unreal today for an original metal 1940 Ford Coupe Deluxe. My first car was a popular one around the beach. Several guys in school wanted to drive it, trading me their car for the day. But I didn't do that too much. Billy was the only friend I let drive mine a few times while I drove his car. I had such a grand time cruising the beach and going places on the weekends with my friends. The cars of the 40s and 50s were great and sturdy cars for teens.

After returning to San Diego, life wasn't quite the same. I'd changed some and missed out on being with everyone I had known and grown up with since second grade. It was only a month and a half until graduation, and all my friends and classmates were excited for the end of the year and its senior festivities. The annual was pretty much done, so I managed to have a picture in it although I hadn't been a part of any senior events all year.

Also, I had no idea right away what all my friends were up to, what they were planning to do after school, or who they were dating or with whom they were going to the senior prom. We'd all continued with our lives, only in different places with different people. Now I was miles away from all I had gotten to know and do for almost a year and back to where I'd been since second grade. It was an adjustment that all worked out, though. I did go to the prom, after prom, and life went on.

I enjoyed being back in San Diego, and having the last of my senior year with everyone I had known for so long, but I didn't have a direction like when I was in Kansas where my classmates seemed to study, work, plan, and make decisions for the future more.

I had applied to Kansas State University in Manhattan and the University of Kansas in Lawrence and been accepted at both before we moved back to California in April of my senior year.

That was not fun. I had made friends and was having a great year in Kansas by then when a two-year move turned out to be just eight months and a return to San Diego, and all I had missed the last nine months. Now, I was graduating with my original senior class only I had not been there for the whole year and everyone was preparing for prom and all the festivities of graduation with about 10 weeks or less of school left for the year.

It was great to be home but awkward at the same time. Much like when I went abroad later in life.

My world had changed; I didn't fit in like before as all goes on without you when you are not in the same place and you change, too, depending

on where you go and who you are. Two of my closest girlfriends were pregnant at 16, chose to keep
their babies and take on all that comes with those
choices.

One was my friend, Kate, who I ran away
from home with in middle school. She wanted to
run away because her dad was an alcoholic and it
upset her a lot. There weren't as many alternatives
for young women then; the alternatives weren't the
best either.

Others I knew faced the same circumstance
but went to Mexico with their mothers and on their
own, which was dreadfully scary. No one's parents
I knew seemed to have talked about these issues
or other women's issues with their daughters. My
close friends didn't talk about whether they were
sexually active or not, and most didn't mention
anything about any other problems they had at
home or at school. Our parents' generation stayed
married no matter what and swept any problems
under the rug for appearance sake. No one talked
about their problems; they bore the brunt of consequences themselves, and some children suffered.

Most of my friends' fathers were military officers in one of the branches of the military who

served in WWII and/or the Korean War. I am sure they suffered from what we now know as PTSD; however, it hadn't been defined as that then it was shell shock and battle fatigue and we didn't know as much about it.

Everyone copes with such issues in their own way. Two things I've seen that help people cope better are a strong faith and healthy, balanced lifestyle. These reasons advanced the current field of positive psychology greatly the 90's in the U.S. and Western Europe to rectify results.

The world appeared to be having plenty more serious problems those days, and our generation for the most part wanted to change and solve them. Many didn't handle much of what was happening well, although the culmination of all that happened during those times created the momentum for change.

It was a difficult and historical time of change for a huge generation of Baby Boomers, even though most us were just teenagers.

I was a senior in high school in physiology class when we heard of JFK's assassination. It seemed unreal coming over the loud speaker. I remembered having seen him at the U.S. Grant Hotel in downtown San Diego when he was running for president and I shook his hand at 15 years old.

He was so young and handsome and seemed like a president I could relate to at that time; then he was dead. The times just got worse and so many leaders were killed. What a cost – so many wondered would it ever really change for the better? Later in the early 21st century, the sixties and early seventies would come to be known and written about as the Consciousness and Sexual Revolution.

Vice President Lyndon B. Johnson was sworn into office as president aboard Air Force One an hour after JFK died and would serve out the remaining 425 days of JFK's term. After that, he was elected president in 1964.

The Vietnam War continued. As the sixties progressed, there were turbulent times on many fronts, and challenging ones as well. Sex, drugs, and rock and roll became the sign of the times as well unrest and peaceful, non-violent protests, though there was violence by many, including the police and others in authority.

The South, with its black oppression and many deaths, continued to give rise to the Civil Rights Movement. By the early sixties, it was in full swing. With more marked incidents in the South, the assassination of Medgar Evers in July 1963, before President Kennedy was killed in November, the generation was alarmed and puzzled.

The assassinations continued in 1965 with Malcolm X, and in 1968 with Dr. Martin Luther King, Jr. and Robert Kennedy. In December 1969, the selective service held two lotteries to determine the order to call for military service. Men born between 1944 and 1950 of the Baby Boomer generation – our brothers, classmates, and friends, were the first to be called to war. Protests and unrest continued.

The music of the time both here and abroad spoke of all that was taking place on the world stage. In the U.S., concerts both indoors and outdoors became the events of the day with many groups and songwriters appearing, singing songs that documented happenings here as well as abroad, and the youth listened just like they do today.

"Musician Bob Dylan wrote his song, *Only a Pawn in Their Game,* about the assassination of Medgar W. Evers in 1963. Nina Simone wrote and sang, *Mississippi Goddam,* about the Evers case, and Phil Ochs wrote the songs, *Another Country* and *Too Many Martyrs,* also titled, *The Ballad of Medgar Evers,* in response to the killing" (https://en.wikipedia.org/wiki/Medgar_Evers).

Eudora Welty's 1963 short story, *Where is the Voice Coming From,* in which the speaker is the imagined assassin of Medgar Evers, was published in The New Yorker. Events escalated, as we all watched on TV.

Television hadn't been around long in the early sixties, and most stations were in black and white, not color, unless your family could afford color. Most news was local, mainly, or covered the state you lived in and its neighboring cities and maybe a major weather event was mentioned, but all wasn't interconnected globally as it is today.

Beginning to see the Vietnam War, assassinations televised and ensuing events like the riots in the South televised where men and women were killed, captured, tortured, and beaten was appalling to us – the youth due to televised exposure creating wider awareness.

The teenagers and young adult Baby Boomers weren't reading the news or listening just to radio news like their parents' and grandparents' generations. Now they saw and knew the truth behind the music sung, and news presented on TV.

The Consciousness Expansion and Counter-culture in the 1960s and beyond, along with the Sexual Revolution and Feminism from 1960 to 1980, was in full swing.

Chapter Three

_____

Marriage and College

It was the spring of 1964 when my mother and I went to several university teas, on tours and interviewed with a few universities once back in San Diego. The University of San Diego was not the varied university it is now in San Diego. UCSD was a private school. Even though those were not out of the question, we considered and looked at a few in Northern California as well and thought about others too. My father and mother both wanted us all to go onto university. Since I was the first child to graduate high school, they expected me then to go to a university as they had, live in the dorms and maybe even join a sorority.

However, just getting home I was not as eager to go away to school again so soon, and what I wanted to do with my life. It was April of the year I was to graduate high school, with fall approaching quickly. Southern California at the beach with its laid-back vibe didn't have the studious environment of the Midwest, what with the ocean and surf culture coming into vogue, to say nothing of the sixties and all that was happening.

Except for the social aspects, I had thought school was boring; the subjects didn't peak my interests or challenge me. I also didn't understand the advantages school offered back then and here in California there didn't seem to be a culture of studying much as there was in Kansas.

In Kansas, my focus as to what I truly wanted to do was beginning to come to the forefront, but once back in San Diego with the ocean and all the outdoor fun, that soon dissipated at the young age of just 17.

I didn't want to go back to Kansas for college, so I was off to San Diego Mesa Community College in the fall. Once there, it wasn't at all what I had imagined college to be like.

My father had gone to William and Mary in Virginia, mother had attended Wellesley and UCLA, and NanaLou North Dakota and Boston University to obtain two degrees. I had heard all my life about going to college and getting my degree, since my dad was an only child and hadn't finished due to taking on the responsibility to help his folks with my only Grandpa, so ill with heart problems, then dad was off to WWII.

My father tried everything to get all four of us to go to college and we didn't until later much to his dismay. I didn't realize the value of going right through and getting a graduate degree back then or know who I was truly was at 17. I felt I could transfer to San Diego State College or go to another state university or private college here in California or elsewhere once I completed my transfer credits, the first two years giving me plenty of time to decide exactly what I really wanted to study and where.

Back in California, school didn't seem to have the appeal it had when I lived in Kansas where so many of my friends were serious about it and had already decided where to go. Here in San Diego, many were going off to college, others were having babies, some were taking a year or two off and traveling to Europe or Hawaii to see more of the world.

Several friends from high school were attending junior college, so I knew a few people, though we didn't see each other much when college began. Mesa reminded me of a high school with ashtrays, as many people smoked back then. I guess it should have been obvious to me. What an awful, smelly habit and to think it was allowed and accepted as cool then. This to me is inspirational as things do change albeit some more slowly than others. I did meet old and make new friends once more at community college.

One of the many people I met and got to know attending Mesa was Woody. His friends nicknamed him that because of his car, a 1946 Ford Woody. He had started taking classes at Mesa like I had that fall. He had been in the Coast Guard up and down the West Coast and Alaska, and got out in 1964 to come home and help his mom.

He was four years older than I when he began at Mesa. As I began seeing him more often, I learned he hadn't grown up in a family anything like mine, yet I didn't realize just how different that was or how it had shaped him. I was charmed with all he had done, seen, and continued to do, as it seemed adventurous to me at the time.

Coming from the same family background and having the same values, I didn't realize made a difference. At 17, I thought I was so grown up. The naïve choices I made as a teenager stemmed from my not knowing much about the opposite sex or relationships, along with being young and not talked to about them. I hadn't learned and gained any understanding about such things.

My parents had known each other all through school, first through 12th grades, and were great friends who hung out with the same group of friends. All the young men knew each other and all the girls knew each other and through their school years they all would did things together and during the summers saw each other until they all went off to colleges somewhere. They even saw many of them afterward and knew their families once some married and had children and kept in touch.

My parents went back east for their 50th high school reunion to their hometown of Palmer. Several of their friends came to visit them during the years we lived in California. I had met many of their school friends over the years.

My parents didn't discuss problems or disagreements about issues in front of any of us if they had them, which I'm sure they did as that is just what relationships are about – different perspectives and beliefs based on how we are brought up. Their deeply rooted faith and principles were the same.

Even though my parents both provided a great foundation, they were both only children, as my mother's only sister died when she was just eight, so she pretty much grew up as an only child with a single mom. They grew up in the same small town albeit from different sides of the tracks, with different socioeconomic backgrounds. They had the same values and etiquette, as did most of their generation. They also lived through the Great Depression as very young children, then WWII as young adults.

In the U.S. after WWII, it was a different time. The industrial urbanization and transportation advances allowed people to move into suburban areas and not be as connected to the rural agricultural centers as in centuries before.

Many of my ancestors had traveled in their day to other places, yet my family was the first of our ancestral generations that settled far from the Northeast in the Southwest. Southern California was great growing up; I didn't truly know what a wonderful place it was to grow up until much later in life, after much travel and living in quite a few places in the world as an adult. The old saying, 'You never realize what you have until it's gone,' comes to mind.

My father's philosophy through most of my second to 12th grade school years seemed to be, "Because I said so." There wasn't much discussion about what he said "no" to and why wasn't a question I asked very often. My dad was away in Korea the first few years in San Diego. After the war, he worked first as a fireman, then at General Dynamics and that was shift work, so my mother didn't work and was home to do for us. Dad was at work sometimes during the week when working shifts when we were all home, so having time with him varied often until it coincided with our school and activity schedules.

He was strict and wanted the very best for us always, as did my mother. They were great and did the best they knew how as we as parents all do. There is no guidebook to go by except the one we learn from our own parents, unless we study and research experts in the field of parenting.

My mother's only sister died when she was eight years old. She never had other siblings, as my NanaLou never remarried. My mother also lost her father when she was just 13. NanaLou was 40 when my mother was born and 53 when her husband died. NanaLou was a domineering woman, who was of a generation when children were to be seen and not heard.

My mother took up art and music to pass the alone times growing up after her sister, Mary, died. She was very talented and artistic at many things, and taught my sister and me a great deal in that respect. Susie is quite artistic in her own right and makes beautiful jewelry, cooks, sews, and decorates well. My brothers are both talented, very handy, and can fix almost anything. We were blessed to learn a lot from our parents and upbringing.

My NanaLou was fortunate the year women got the right to vote, yet all women were still not allowed to vote then; there were geographical exceptions for many in the U.S. and globally for many years to come. Women before then had to have permission from their fathers and/or husbands to even continue their education. Women were only educated to take up their expected social role as housewives and mothers.

A great modern example of this is the movie, *Mona Lisa Smile* (2003), which stars Julia Roberts, a freethinking art professor from the West Coast who teaches girls to question their traditional social roles when she goes against the norm as a new professor at Wellesley College challenging her students to pursue their dreams and not settle only on the social norms of the times.

Woody and I saw each other not only at school and with a myriad of friends at the beach and parties on the weekends since many of my girlfriends and his friends hung around together. I had my 1940 Ford Coupe, went to school, worked part-time, and liked seeing him as often as I had time to do so.

He was busy taking care of his mom's house, working, going to school, and surfing, which he loved. He also spent hours taking care of his 1946 Ford Woody, hence his nickname. We ended up dating steadily that first year or so of college.

I was smitten! I thought I was in love and very naïve at just 17 when it came to what I thought was a serious relationship. Truth be told I was smitten with his charm, allure of his adventures, freedom, experience and in over my head before I knew what was happening.

Life was busy and school was going well. I worked as hostess at a restaurant part-time for gas money and extras I wanted since I was still living at home. Weekends came and went. Woody and his friends would take off up the coast some weekends to surf and several of them went to Mazatlán, Mexico, surfing each year over the Christmas holidays.

Most of his friends were older than I and he was four years older than me, so even the girls I met with them all were a few years older than me. I did meet several other girls I graduated high school with and hadn't known too well who knew young men Woody's age that were in that group for road and surf trips. Several of them rented homes while going to college and working now that they were out of high school. They would have weekend parties at their places. Woody lived in his mom's house, so he had parties, too, but didn't have any roommates.

In the Coast Guard, he had been up and down the West Coast to Alaska and down to Mexico back before there was an airport in Puerto Vallarta when it was still a small, fishing village. Elizabeth Taylor and Richard Burton hadn't made it famous with their film, *The Night of the Iguana*.

The West Coast wasn't a stranger to him, and I wanted to go, too. There was no way my dad was allowing me to do that, and it was mainly a guy's trip anyway. It seemed so exciting! I had always dreamed of traveling the world to see all its different people and places, but what I hadn't learned yet was one needed to have the means to do that, an Ivy League education, profitable, entrepreneurial endeavor or marriage was key.

Christmas of 1965 we got engaged a little over a year after we met. My parents never said anything to me about not liking Woody or spoke to me about why a long-term relationship may not be best for us. I hadn't met his parents yet, but I did meet his foster mom and knew her two children. She was a single mom with a clothing store in town that my girlfriends and I would shop in from time to time when in high school.

Her son, Bill, also went into the Coast Guard; they were best friends and still are today. I really liked him, too. Her daughter, Diane, was beautiful. Ginny was a great lady. Woody's parents were divorced too. When his mom, who had custody, was hospitalized years earlier, he and his brother, Jay, went into the foster system, but Ginny offered to take Woody. That was special and so good for him. I liked her and both her children, who were older than me.

Looking back today, I believe my dad was more concerned about our being together, wheth-

er we'd both finish school, and if Woody would
be able to support the lifestyle and type of family
my dad knew I wanted. He talked to Woody often,
knew it was hard to work nights and go to school
during the day, so offered to pay his college expenses if he was serious about finishing his university
degree. Woody had been on his own so long and in
the military like my dad, but that never happened.
Woody was four years older than me and for whatever reasons, that hadn't appealed to him. Maybe it
was because he had never really had a male figure
in his life other than his older brother and was used
to doing things on his own terms or by himself.

We married earlier than planned the next
year and I had our first son, Will, soon after. Being
pregnant was easy. I had no problems, and I loved
being a mom. What a wake-up call being a mother
was, though, as I didn't know much about nutrition
at the time being a teenager and Will had colic. A
baby with colic is miserable, so I was miserable too.
Neither of us got much sleep, Woody wasn't into
taking on many of the chores involved with being a
father, other than working and school.

No one seemed to have any answers for me.
My mother didn't have any suggestions, and her

best friend who was a registered nurse didn't either. There was no Google and Internet as a resource to look anything up. So those first few months were difficult.

Will was born in late October so Halloween happened right away and Woody went partying with others, much to my dismay. I should admit I was bothered and somewhat jealous too.

Then came the holidays and a myriad of parties. We seemed to manage through many disagreements, as I learned motherhood is the woman's responsibility, at least it seemed, and nobody else's.

Will outgrew colic, thankfully. He was a good little boy, smart and active and my joy. Woody took a more active role with him as he got older and could walk and go with him. Woody wanted a cheaper form of transportation to school and work, so he bought a Harley-Davidson Sportster.

I would roller skate with Will in the stroller along the sea wall to my parents' home in Crown Point when I had the chance and his dad had to work or was doing other things like working on his car, surfing, or helping friends. Many of the girls I knew had married and we met other couples that Woody had known and people from school we had met, and being at the beach there was always much to do on weekends: going to the shore, barbecues. A game called Over-the-Line began in Mission Beach in the 1950s and Woody played in it many times. It continues to thrive today on a much larger scale.

My mother-in-law, Woody's mom, was home living in her own home, and we lived above her in a studio that they had previously rented. It was great, and she would babysit Will for us often. She was a lifesaver, as was my mom since they were all tickled pink to have their first grandbaby.

My siblings loved Will to pieces, too, and helped once he was only 18 months old. The summer passed quickly, and I planned to be able to get back to school soon to complete that second year to finish and transfer to San Diego State for my bachelor's degree. It kept me busy what with working part-time, cooking dinners, and doing homework. It was nice to have the bigger place with Little Mom downstairs to hang out, cook dinner, do homework, and let Will run around. She enjoyed it.

My oldest brother, Davey, was drafted in 1967, as were many of our classmates, friends, and others. Many who served had come home to unsettled times and ill receptions while too many others were killed. For the first time in history due to TV, a war could be televised; it was broadcast nightly on the news stations.

Back then, technology wasn't anything like it is today. There were no cell phones, so actually talking via Facetime to brothers or parents, men and women who were overseas was impossible.

Watching the news and seeing those in uniform who might be family members and classmates that you knew had gone seemed surreal. My parents were getting cassette tapes from my brother, Davey, from Vietnam. I know it must have been hard for my mother to think of her son overseas after living through WWII and so many like my dad that she knew being overseas and many of them didn't return. My father was one of the lucky ones, he always said. While Davey was overseas, my mother brought my NanaLou out to California.

NanaLou had fallen, her caregiver found her, and my mother got the news from the hospital back east. NanaLou was in her late 80s and still living in her own home with a caregiver/housekeeper, who came every day to stay with her, cook, clean, and keep her company along with bringing all in to meet her needs.

Mom and NanaLou spoke often on the phone, and they still wrote letters, as well. NanaLou was perfectly lucid, well, and her handwriting and letters were impeccable. However, her caregiver didn't come on the weekends and for whatever reason unbeknownst to anyone my NanaLou decided to go to the cellar and fell. She hadn't broken anything but remained there for a time until her caregiver found her early Monday morning. She called help and they got Nana to the hospital and phoned my mother.

At the hospital, they found she had cancer throughout her body that had evidently begun in her breast years before. No one knew this and she had taken care of it herself and much to the doctors' astonishment she was not in any pain.

My parents flew back east to bring her back to California; I remember my mother calling me to tell me what had happened, when they would be back, and where she had arranged for her to stay when they returned. It had been 13 years since I last saw my NanaLou, when she was 75. She was almost 88 now and coming to California to live out the rest of her life.

In the hospital while cared for and examined by the doctors, the good news was they found she hadn't broken anything – thankfully. She only had minor bruises, and was dirty from the soil and coal dust on the cellar floor. She was also upset. Considering her age and cancer diagnosis, the doctors back east had given her roughly six months or so to live.

Once my mother got NanaLou to California and in a nursing home in La Jolla, I went with my mother to visit right away. It was good to see my NanaLou again. It had been so long. She looked well and as I remembered her, only frailer. She'd only been here a few days. My mother went each day to check on her and visit.

They didn't have her dressed yet, except in a hospital gown. As the nurses got her out of bed to take her to the bathroom, her gown fell open and from where I sat I glimpsed her chest where once was a breast was now an open wound. She had been taking care of herself with poultices and such for some time as far as I recall without medical assistance.

Her brother, Uncle Walter in Minneapolis, remember had been a medical doctor who tended to their sister, Aunt Mamie, so NanaLou, who outlived them both, had inherited all his medical instruments when he passed. That picture of her chest is still in my head to this day and furthered my interest in preventive medicine and nutrition, as that happening to me is not something I wanted to think about occurring in my later life if there were ways to avert it.

In the fall of 1968, a little over a year after Davey went to Vietnam, I got a call from my mother that he was shot, then she broke into tears. I was horrified! She didn't tell me what happened before she started crying – my mind immediately thought, "Oh my God! What if he's terribly hurt or dead!"

She regained her composure and explained what she had been told. Davey was alive! Praise GOD! He was blessed that the bullet went right through his leg, missing all the bones and major arteries and lodged in his other leg. Next, he was air lifted and taken to Osaka, Japan to be treated and would be sent home. Now we had to wait.

What a fright, but thank God, he was alive. God bless all those who served, serve, came home, went missing, were wounded, gave their lives, and to all the families who lost loved ones. We are so indebted to them all for the freedoms we enjoy each day. We waited and wondered when Davey would get back home.

It seemed to take quite a long time, especially without the instant communication means we have today. It was moving toward the holidays and we were all anxious.

We all waited while we all enjoyed spending time getting to know Nanalou and seeing her more often. Mom had moved her earlier to a nicer place in La Jolla, the Cloisters, where Frances, my mother's long-time friend and neighbor when we first moved into Crown Point, worked as a nurse. NanaLou loved it there.

NanaLou was tickled to see us all, and she loved the boys and men and lit up when they came. She met Will and even got to hold John shortly after he arrived the spring of 1969 – four generations – how special! Her visits were a treat for us all.

My NanaLou was an interesting lady. She was blessed with having no pain, didn't have to take pain medication and lived much longer than the six months' doctors back east had given her. She passed before Davey returned home.

Finally, Davey was flown into San Diego to the Balboa Veterans Hospital close to the San Diego Zoo. It was almost Thanksgiving and everyone with any rank was on vacation for the upcoming holidays.

I had a hard time getting in contact with someone to sign a release to get him discharged and home to us. It was so great to have him back. He stayed with us at the beach until mom and dad got back home, as they went when they had Nanalou's body flown back to Massachusetts to be buried in the family plot next to her father and sister in Monson before the ground was frozen and the snow fell.

Woody and Davey talked and he relaxed some, although it was hard for him. I was glad to have been able to get him out of the hospital and bring him home. I remember him telling me he saw Bob Hope while he was in the hospital in Japan, as he had visited the service men there.

Later when my mom and I were visiting, I remember her telling me about that last day she had gone to visit her mother. She said they had a nice long visit and it was getting close to supper time, NanaLou warmly told her you need to get home for supper with David and the children, as I will be

with your sister and father tonight. She died peace-
fully that evening.

After Johnson did not run for a second term in
1968, Nixon was elected president. It was the late
sixties, and they hadn't yet become more peaceful
times. The music of the day continued to reflect the
times. Nixon approved our incursion into Cambo-
dia in 1970; protests of the war escalated on many
college campuses that led to the Kent State shoot-
ings known as the May 4th Massacre. Life went on
although the times seemed to be so conflicted.

I had met another couple with Woody, Terry
and Carolyn, and others that he had known previously from living at the beach, surfing, being in
the Coast Guard, and before at high school. We enjoyed going to dinner with Terri and Carolyn and
although she was two years or so older than I was
we got along well. She and Terry didn't have any
children, so they could go and do as they pleased
together. They invited us to go to Ensenada to the
hot springs and we did a of times and to the Gulf
side of Baja California.

Those were fun trips and I enjoyed them. They
were living in Pacific Beach and wanted to move
to South Mission Beach, so we all decided to rent a

bigger house across the street from Little Mom and live together to share expenses.

The studio was getting cramped and we would still be close to Little Mom. Very soon that didn't work out well at all; the three of them seemed to party together often while I stayed home. Much of the time that was fine as I went along to the beach with everyone and in the evening when little Mom babysat Will. It changed as they were all older than me and many times kept the party going into the evening hours at the beach bars that I couldn't get into yet or they all got together later when I couldn't join them.

I later learned that Carolyn was sleeping with Woody. I took Will and moved back into my parents' house heartbroken. I always wanted to be happily married forever like my parents. I still loved him, and it didn't seem fair. I filed for divorce, but didn't like being single again. And I would run into Woody or he would see me around town during the day or on the weekends, follow me, and want to talk. It made it even harder as I wanted my marriage and family to all work. I switched jobs and tried to get on with my life.

I started working full-time as a receptionist for Dillingham Corporation in Sorrento Valley. It was a great job; I met nice people. Thad was the VP from Hawaii and his family owned the company. If I remember correctly, he had just graduated college and was sent to run the new office in San Diego.

I also met a man from Australia, Richard, who was a professional scuba diver and his father ran the Sydney office. His Australian accent over the phone sounded to me like he was drunk so I hung up on him a lot as I had never met him in person at the office.

He finally came in one day and stopped at my desk to ask that I stop hanging up on him when he called the office. I was so embarrassed! Anyway, he and Thad were close friends being from other places, yet connected through business and in San Diego now.

They were both very nice men. I liked them both, and they would invite me to get-togethers on the weekends. I ended up spending time with them both on occasion, once to celebrate Thad's uncle's 63rd birthday; he was in town from Honolulu.

Richard was always somewhere diving in the world, like in the Azores off Portugal. He asked me to dinner a few times and to go swimming with him. I took up scuba diving and got certified. We all had a great time together, and they were wonderful, polite gentlemen whose company I enjoyed.

But intermittently, Woody would happen to run into me and one night we saw each other, stopped to talk over everything, he missed us, and I missed him and being a family together. We ended up staying the night together that for me as time moved forward ended up proving to be another unwise choice. But I have no regrets and three beautiful, grown children from that relationship and lessons learned about who I am – my true self.

Woody and I decided to give our marriage another go. He had gone right onto San Diego State University while I stayed home with Will, and I still had to finish courses I hadn't completed yet. I barely completed them this time as that night I stayed with Woody I got pregnant with our second son, John, who was born in May, right during finals. I had to track down my oceanography professor whose final I missed while giving birth. He allowed me to make it up, and I passed. Now I could transfer all credits and register to attend San Diego State once John was a little older. Eventually, we both would be at San Diego State, even though having the boys had slowed me down.

Woody had taken the year off when we weren't together and worked to save money. He had only completed a course or two, so he started back slowly with a couple courses for the beginning semester of that junior year. He had decided to major in anthropology. His first anthropology class was working to excavate a site near the Mission San Diego de Acalá in Presidio Park.

In that class, he met a fellow classmate, Tom, and they became fast friends. Tom was married with a daughter who was just two years old. Tom invited us to come to his home in Fallbrook to meet his family. We went up on the weekend to visit, and I met his wife, Vera. She and I became fast friends. I liked her immediately and several of her friends who lived there, too.

Later in 1969, after visiting quite a bit more, Woody wanted to move up to Fallbrook, so we did. We had outgrown South Mission Beach, what with the parking problems, and he could work in the avocado businesses of friends and go to school with Tom two days a week to finish his degree. Tom was already driving 100 miles one way on Tuesdays and Thursdays to attend classes, so it would work well for him. Vera worked at the dental office and part-time at Head Start, which was great because Will started preschool there and he knew Vera well.

I tried to stay in school two days a week and ride along with Woody and Tom once John was older, but it just didn't work for me because when I was home with the family there was too much to do along with my studies. I didn't have the extra energy needed to do all for school, as well without more help.

I decided to wait until the boys were older, then I could return and complete my degree. Life was good and Woody's mom, Eleanor, came up often to stay and see the boys. She liked the quiet, rural atmosphere of a small town and, of course, staying with us. I enjoyed her help immensely.

Little Mom, Eleanor (as the boys called her since she was shorter than my mom and both their names were hard for them to say), had been self-committed to the state hospital since she was 23 diagnosed with paranoid schizophrenia.

When I first learned this after having Will, it frightened me. I didn't know much about it then, and I learned much more and that it usually develops more in men and less often in women but not until the early 20s. This to me was even worse than the diseases that afflicted my grandmothers, as I couldn't imagine having beautiful, healthy, strong boys who got sick later with this awful disease; especially when I saw over the years what it had done to this attractive, wonderful mother-in-law of mine.

Also, if she stayed on a higher protein diet and away from ice cream and sugars, she was much better and didn't seem to have as many episodes. It was better when she was with us and not home alone. In South Mission Beach when I first had Will, her social worker told me it would help and be healthy for her to be around us and focus and help with her grandson more, we jumped at that opportunity. It benefited us all. I got a full-time job at the telephone company as a long-distance operator for Pacific Bell and Woody also worked, so she watched Will when he was little during the day.

Then I would cook dinner, and she didn't mind cleaning up. I always made extras so she had lots to eat during the day that was healthy and we kept sweets out of the house. She was the best au pair, a jewel, and Will was always extremely close to her. She was my first real interest in nutritional health and wellness that I think had really been cultivated in my subconscious mind due to Grandpa Davis being so ill and knowing my mom's dad and sister had passed.

Children are so inquisitive about people and question those things. Also, I had always known that my father was interested in medicine and becoming a doctor, but felt obligated to take care of his parents as an only child and hadn't gone onto medical school what with WWII happening and all.

Once when Little Mom was staying with us, Woody and I had the chance to go with his brother, Jay, and his girlfriend at that time, to Mexico. Jay was driving to Puerto Vallarta then onto Belize City in British Honduras to look at land to buy in the Orange Walk District. I had always wanted to go to Mexico ever since I met Woody and his friends.

Little Mom agreed to stay at our house in Fallbrook and watch the boys. Will was in kindergarten and Dan was just over two years old. I was so excited that we could go. Traveling the world and seeing all its people had been a dream of mine since I was very young.

What a fantastic trip! I loved it! The food was wonderful, as were the beaches, countryside, and small fishing villages and towns.

Gloria, Jay's girlfriend who came along, flew back to Los Angeles from Puerto Vallarta for work. We covered so many of the western states of Mexico: Sonora, Sinaloa, Nayarit, on our drive down to Jalisco. Our days in Puerto Vallarta on the beaches were heavenly.

The three of us were off again toward the Yucatan and parts south. Woody wanted to see all the archaeological ruins he had studied along the way.

Upon leaving Jalisco, we headed for Michoacán away from the beach inland toward Mexico City. We stopped and ate and saw things all along the way but pretty much kept moving. In Mexico City, we spent time to see the city of Teotihuacán with its 10 pyramids that was built between A. D. 1 and 250 by the Inca and has been compared to the ancient city of Rome.

Its largest pyramid is the Pyramid of the Sun. Also impressive was the Museo Nacional de Antropología e Historia that I could've stayed in for a week or more. It was so interesting and filled with such a wonderful history of Mexico and its peoples.

Then we were off through Puebla, Oaxaca, and stopping in Chiapas to see the Mayan ruins of Palenque. Pakal the Great, king of Maya Palenque, initiated the building of the Temple of the Inscriptions at Palenque to be used as the tomb. It was not discovered until 1952, so seeing it not long after was amazing.

The pyramids of southern Mexico and Central America were also used as temples and places for navigation among the Mayans more than 3,000 years ago.

In Central America, the immense waterfalls, surrounding fields outside town that we could park our GMC van in with other tourists, was great. The jungles of Chiapas were so lush and interesting, as were the Vaqueros who rode herd on the Brahman cattle each evening through the fields to take them to other pastures. They were magnificent as they shouted to the bulls and led them via horseback where they wanted them to go. It was an awesome image at dusk.

Onward through Tabasco, Campeche, Veracruz, to more Mayan sites in the Yucatán and the

Quintana Roo – my favorite along the Caribbean – WOW! In early 1972, the beaches were bare except for the local Conch fisherman. We bought fish to cook for dinner over campfire on the beach. There were mounds of shells also, so I got one to take home. We slept under the stars in hammocks tied to palm trees. We swam in the turquoise waters of the ocean and walked along the pure, white-sand beaches.

I will never forget the ruins of Chichén Itzá on the Yucatan and Tulum on Quintana Roo with hardly a soul around. We were free to roam through them at our leisure and see all as we lolled for days in that area.

These were some of the most beautiful beach areas I have ever seen in the world although now they have changed so much that it makes those times then even more spectacular.

We headed down to the ruins in Chetumal, Mexico, and didn't make it into Belize because we got a flat tire on Jay's van and were unable to find a spare to fit it besides the one we had and used, so Jay decided with the long trip home we best head that way.

Our trip had been grand and so awesome that I felt blessed and didn't mind. I had hoped I could come back one day, as the traditional clothing of the women reminded me of my trip across our Indian lands when I was seven to visit my grandparents.

Every village was different and the women wore traditional clothing. I met a lady from the states while we were briefly in Oaxaca on our way home again who shared her adventures in Guatemala and showed me some of the women's traditional Huipilas she had bought there. I remember thinking they were so pretty, all hand woven and artistically embroidered and done with natural dyes.

Coming back one day again with Vera and my sister to see all and shop, too, would be grand. On this trip, the girlie times Gloria and I spent in shops, looking at clothing, jewelry, art, crafts, and places of interest stopped when Gloria left for L.A, from Puerto Vallarta.

Jay and Woody were on a mission to see the ruins and land, which was the trip's purpose. I was along for the ride. They drove, as it was difficult when it got dark, with animals on the highways and checkpoints every now and again. I didn't want to drive, so I assisted with meals, washed out clothes, and organized the van, so we traveled farther and were able to stop and see and do all we figured out ahead of time to do.

Coming back one day again with my sister and sisters-of-the-heart to see all the things women love and to shop would be great. I was happy doing so and being along on the trip. It was a once-in-a-lifetime adventure and I was thankful the whole time!

It was so amazingly different from the U.S. and such a learning experience for me. What I didn't know at that time is I would get to travel to Mexico several more times; I have been truly blessed!

Jay, Woody and I made it home and loved being back. The boys and Little Mom were happy we were home and to see us. We had been gone almost a month. Not too long after we got home, we had the chance to move into a bigger house just outside of town where we'd all have more room.

Vera's sister, DeeDee, was renting it and wanted to move into town, so she and I decided to trade the houses we rented. Woody was working for Rainbow Organics, and it wasn't any farther for him to work or to meet Tom for school Tuesdays and Thursdays. DeeDee took our house, and we took hers. We were all happy with the arrangement.

Chapter Four

Through It All Life Happens

My brother, Davey, had married and they had a son. My brother had opened his own carpet laying business in Fallbrook and was doing great. Susie was 20 and living with her boyfriend, Danny, nearby. Our parents had sold their home in Crown Point and moved inland to the new community of Rancho Bernardo close to Poway with our youngest brother, Ned, where he continued high school, played football, and graduated from Poway High.

Susie and Danny lost the house they had rented and asked if they could move in with us. We agreed, so they did. We fixed up the house with the landlord's permission and painted and hung wallpaper and got it all decorated nice and it looked great. A little later, after talking about Mexico quite a bit with my sister and Vera, who lived presently in Tucson, the three of us decided to go, as I had dreamt of doing since I last visited.

Vera invited another lady, Claudia, and the four of us along with my boys and Vera's daughter and our husbands' blessings all went from Nogales, Arizona, on the train to Mexico City and beyond to Guatemala City then back home. What an amazing trip that was and it's an adventurous story for yet another later book.

Not long after Susie and I returned home with my boys, she and Danny found a new house of their own, but Susie left a few large furniture items with us because they didn't have room at their new place.

Vera had left some things with me too when she, Tom, and their daughter had moved to Tucson after Tom had graduated and gotten a job there at the University of Arizona in Tucson excavating archaeological sites in Arizona.

We left from Nogales, since they were there and the train to Mexico City ran straight through from Nogales, Arizona. What a trip we all still relish talking to each other about as adults and our children and Vera and I are still the best friends and will be forever as are our children.

What a blessing that is after all these years; I'm so thankful!

The house seemed empty but the boys would soon be in school and now they each had their own room. It was great and Woody was not in school. He had dropped out his senior year and I hadn't gone back yet.

Woody was working seven days a week and we were both busy with family and life. I had made the boys each five new cowboy shirts for the school year as summer was almost over. I had bought backpacks and school supplies, and Dan was ready for kindergarten and Will would be in third grade. He was going to play baseball and was excited! He loved sports and did well in school.

Woody and I hadn't had a night out in months it seemed, so Sunday evening, September 9th, we decided to go visit friends we hadn't seen in quite some time. We loaded up the car and put the boys in their pajamas so they would be ready to fall asleep in the car and go right to bed if it got late.

It was a warm wonderful evening and off we went. Our friends weren't home, so we went onto the theater to see Judge Roy Bean and Father Sun Sister Moon. On our way home, we saw lots of flashing, red lights as we got closer to the house.

Upon driving up the driveway, we saw firemen, and the house was destroyed.

What a shock! Where were we going to stay that night? Now I don't even remember where we stayed. I do remember how thankful I was that we were all alive and not harmed. Only things were lost, which are irreplaceable, not lives. God is good!

We learned how blessed we truly were to live in the U.S. where family and many friends help when you're in need and there is such an abundance of stuff. What a blessing! As Americans, we are so fortunate. It was such a FREE feeling for me as well, like I could do, go and start over anywhere, so that is just what we slowly did.

For the next three years, it was grand in many ways. We found a terrific, 80-acre place to homestead for free. After losing all with no renter's insurance at the time, it gave us the chance to start fresh. The new place was perfect for the boys to grow up on, run, play, and explore. It was another time of learning lessons for me in the ongoing lifelong learning process of who I truly am.

Once we cleaned it up, repaired, and hooked all up, we could buy it in a few years. It was a challenge in many ways but the land had spring water, live oaks, a few out buildings, and an old adobe house. We bought chickens, goats, a pig, planted a garden, fixed up the cozy little place, and lived well. The boys were off to school and made friends.

As the years passed, being that far out of town and not having the basic conveniences like electricity got to me. Living like *Little House on the Prairie* worked for a few seasons, having fresh eggs and home-grown food. I loved canning and gardening and still do; there is a lot to be said for making your own yogurt, cheeses, and bread.

I was going to have another child and having to go twenty-eight miles one way to do laundry, groceries and staples was getting to be too much. No electricity was a major factor. It was clear even though the landowner offered to sell us the land at an incredible price, my husband was not ever going to buy. He was content with life the way it was there.

Once our daughter, Rosie, was a year and four months old, it just wasn't working for me any longer for a myriad of reasons, so I left. I wanted back the conveniences, comfort, cleanliness of hot water without having to heat it on a stove and a flush toilet. Living five years like little house of the prairie was enough; even though, I cherish that time – family, friends and all the experiences it offered.

I believe, a marriage needs to be a two-way street, reciprocal give and take relationship of communication and compromise for which both continually work. They don't work if not on a solid foundation of like values, appreciation, willingness and desire to ensure it work. Off I moved north to Washington State, closer to my parents who had retired there.

I had no car to take us north and had arranged for a friend of my brothers who was on his way back to Washington after visiting his mother in Crown Point. I'd known Bob since we were all young so he agreed to pick me up down the road and drive Rosie and me to my sister's house near Olympia. I literally had to walk away from all down the road about two miles to meet him.

The most heart wrenching thing I chose to do was leave my sons with their father. I knew he would feed them and hoped they'd stay in school. I prayed they would stay safe and well, forgive me, understand later when grown up why I did what I did. I prayed I'd get to make it up to them and we'd have good relationships as adults and be close.

I always wanted a great marriage like my parents and children too although things don't always go as we hope. My marriage was over now forever. I moved in with my sister, Susie, and began to study to get my real estate license. It worked well. I helped my sister out with all I could, as she was single and worked construction at that time.

We had a good time together as she had lived in Washington for a decade and we hadn't seen much of each other. We got to catch up a lot. My parents visited. But I missed my sons a great deal and being closer. I could call little mom on her land line and Vera, my close friend was back in SoCal and kept in touch too. Even though their dad had no electricity and no phone, those first months in Washington I knew they were in school and alright. Life was moving on for us all.

During the summer, their dad brought them up to visit. It was so wonderful to see them both. Rosie was happy to see them too, and they were both great with her as always. I didn't want to see them go, so we rode back to SoCal with them and Rosie and I stayed with my friend. I'm sure my ex-husband thought I would be staying with them.

After his abuse, I had learned life was good on my own. Anything I worked for was possible to achieve and I wanted more for my children and me. The world was a beautiful place, with kind people and opportunity, and I was going for it "for with God nothing shall be impossible" (Luke 1:37, Life Application Bible KJV).

I decided to stay close, go back to school and finish my degree, so that is just what I did.

Joe, a friend for many years, and I started seeing each other. We were together for several years during which time I completed my degree, got a good job with the county, and had another son, Micah. When Micah was four and Rosie was in first grade, I needed to move back to Washington close to my parents and continue working on the goals I set for my children and me. Joe and I parted on good terms as friends and stayed in touch.

Having begun as a nutrition major, I ended up as an Education major. Then went back to complete the course work I needed to obtain my teaching credential. It was important for me to have the same schedule as my children during the year as a single mom. While doing so, Dan called to ask if he could come live with me. Of course! What an answered prayer, and Woody flew him up. Will had graduated from high school and moved back to the beach with grandma Eleanor, little mom. He was taking a year off after high school before going to university.

Dan joined us all, and I loved it. He stayed with me and his siblings for a while and we got to work through things together and catch up with each other. The piece of property close to my parents that Micah's dad helped us buy had a single wide trailer on it that was too small for us all. My parents asked Dan to stay with them. They had the room and were delighted to have him. It was easier for Dan going back and forth to high school, as the bus came right by their house. My dad was just what he needed during the end of high school and my mother enjoyed taking care of him. They loved having him there and his school friends around and going to his sports events. It was so great for us all and such a blessing since we were all in school. And we know that *all things* work together for *good* to them that love God, …

Dan graduated high school the same year I completed my course work plus teaching credential. We celebrated together and went to visit in SoCal. Dan was going to enlist in the Army – he always wanted to be an Airborne Ranger. He signed up in San Diego and was sent to Fort Benning, Georgia for jump school. Those couple years weren't long enough before he left again, but we were good and I was so proud of him. We talked often.

After college, I got a few teaching jobs in schools that made me rethink becoming a teacher since my passion had always been nutrition. I dreamt of teaching others about health and wellness. I was hired the third year I taught at Rosie and Micah's school and close to family. The end of my first year at Rosie and Micah's school Will graduated from Point Loma Nazarene University. We all flew down to attend the ceremony. We stayed a few days to celebrate with him. Will had done so well. It was bittersweet having to leave again. I was so proud of him.

But too soon we were back home to school and work. I taught at the same school my children attended until Rosie was almost out of high school and Micah was just ready to enter high school. During my tenure, I completed my first Master's degree. I enjoyed teaching and the students, but it was time for a change. We moved so I could take a job teaching college.

It was a new chapter for us all. Dan was chosen out of the Airborne Rangers for The Old Guard and stationed in Washington, D.C. Will had sorted out what he wanted to do and opened his own board shop on the California coast. He was working hard but doing well and loved it. Rosie was graduating and going to go to community college in Spokane with friends. And Micah was enjoying high school sports, and in a couple more years he'd be a graduate as well. For now, it was just the two of us.

Working at the college level was exciting for me. I enjoyed getting to know my colleagues and being able to work in the community as well. Since my Master's degree was in teaching English as a Second/Foreign Language, I taught international students along with US students all areas of English: reading, writing, listening and speaking. I also got to continue my professional development and attend/present at the annual teachers of English to speakers of other languages (TESOL) national conventions and other English conferences.

Rosie didn't stay in Spokane long. Come Christmas break, she asked to come home. I was delighted! She was a great student and good worker, but living with friends just wasn't working for her. She decided to go to college where I worked to finish up her first two years. It was back to the three of us.

The summer of Micah's junior year Rosie completed her transfer credits and decided it was time to move onto bigger venues. She wanted to go to San Diego and live with her big brother, Will, and work for him to gain residency before going on to complete her Bachelor's degree there. Will was all for the plan. We took off on a road trip south just before school started back up in the fall. It was a great chance to visit and get her all settled. We hadn't seen Will's store and visited for a while and were impressed and glad to be able to make the trip. Rosie was a bit overwhelmed with San Diego at first, but after a few weeks she was enjoying getting to know Will and the area more.

It was just Micah and me once again. We had lots to do that year figuring out where he

was going to school and getting that all together. He wanted to be a chef and had always loved to cook. I was contemplating going back to school to complete my doctorate. I couldn't teach at a university without it and I had always wanted to be a doctor. With all my children grown and on my own, I would have the time to do so. I started looking at schools and found a business program that fit. I applied to Fielding Graduate Institute, interviewed in Seattle, and was accepted. I would attend a one-week orientation session in Santa Barbara, California then be able to work mainly online while teaching during the year. Rosie met me in Santa Barbara, and we got to visit for a few days and catch up. Both seeing her and orientation were great! Rosie was happy, in school, working and doing well. I also met so many faculty and doctoral students many of whom would become lasting friends.

Micah and I both were beginning new adventures. He decided he wanted to go to culinary school, and western Washington was close. His best friend from school was going too, so it worked well for the two of them. They moved after graduation, found a nice apartment and jobs. I visited, and he came home for the weekend every now and then. I taught summer school, worked on my doctoral coursework, and life was busy and full.

Always health and wellness remained my passion especially since so much of my vocation was spent on cognitive academic activities. Balance was key for my holistic (mental, emotional, physical and spiritual) wellness. I always belonged to a gym and worked out regularly three to five days a week. I also taught step aerobics in my community and participated in local 3K, 5K and 10K runs on the weekends with friends whenever possible.

The international students I taught also taught me about different foods and modalities they used to improve their health and wellness. I was introduced to Kombucha years ago by Svetlana, my Ukrainian work study student, whose mother grew it. She was kind enough to share one with me, how to care for it and use it. Being a life-long learner is key along with keeping an open mind and trying new things, which I was about to find out again soon.

At the end of my first year of doctoral study, I attended a research session in Denver. Beth, whom I met at orientation earlier and worked in an online course with asked me to come to mainland China to teach. She, her husband and daughter were living and teaching there. I was working and living in Washington. I thought how can I possibly do that; even though, I had always wanted to go abroad and live and work overseas. Another doctoral colleague of ours challenged me – saying you're not going you keep saying if, when, maybe. How can I? She simply said go back to work and ask for a year's leave of absence. I did. It was granted. Three months later I was in mainland China living, teaching at Shenzhen University and working with Beth on our PhDs.

My experiences in China over the next three years were wonderful. I was surprised when Rosie came to live with me just a short two months after I got there. We went home for the summer when the school year ended. Rosie stayed but loved having had the opportunity to live abroad. I decided to stay and work abroad and continue my study, but went home a couple times a year, and spent quality time with family when I did.

I loved being a mother; children are God's greatest gifts and wonderful teachers as well. They were grown now and all doing well. I was so blessed and thankful to have them. It was my time to go, do and become – Dr. Ann. The new relationships and learning opportunities that I encountered both living and working abroad and going through the doctoral program of Fielding Graduate Institute with all its distributed learning opportunities globally were transformative. The wonderful people that became a part of my life and lasting friends whom I shared and learned so much with and from enriched my life. I'm blessed that they still do and new relationships also happen.

The following chapters share more transformative stories, lessons learned and ways of knowing that I've experienced living with myself reflected through my relationships with others. I'm so thankful and blessed to have had many relationships from which to learn about myself. I continue to be a work in progress, and must focus being present - one day at a time. My loving mother told me I was a perpetual student. I realize now that I am most happy being a life-long learner each day of my life who still has much to learn and hopefully some to impart.

Chapter Five

Self-Talk versus Authentic "Real" Dialogue

"Be mindful of your self-talk.
It's a conversation with the universe."
– David James Lees

What is self-talk? I have had inner conversations that refer to the inner dialogues that I have with myself about my social environment, and me. My external conversations, on the other hand, refer to those parts of my internal conversations that I choose to share with others.

We all have some sort of self-generated dialogue taking place privately in our minds. It is your inner voice.

"Most people believe these [dialogues] are beyond their control. Stop and be aware …; no one

knows for sure how these happen in our heads ...."
(www.healthdirect.gov.au/self-talk).

We can recognize and consciously change this self-talk so that it becomes positive most of the time instead of negative. It is up to us to do so!

Self-talk is the inner voice in your head that goes on daily, usually telling you things that aren't true about what you look like and don't like about yourself. It's that ridiculous critic and/or those unrealistic thoughts about what you'd like to have, be, or do in life that if you're not willing to create a plan of action and realistically do the work will not happen.

These are the thoughts that you or I interpret and think about situations, episodes, interactions, and what has happened for the most part incorrectly because we don't ask the people involved any questions to clarify and explain our hurt feelings, misunderstandings, or misinterpretations for us.

It is the working of our brain to process all our neutral, positive, and negative thoughts for understanding all at once for later use. It is otherwise known as *"mind monkey or monkey mind,"* from Chinese (xinyuan) "heart-/mind-monkey," a Buddhist term meaning unsettled; restless; capricious;

whimsical; fanciful; inconstant; confused; indecisive; uncontrollable (google.com).

Gallager (2011) described mind monkeys beautifully, "Buddha described the human mind as being filled with drunken monkeys, jumping around, screeching, chattering, carrying on endlessly. We all have monkey minds, Buddha said, with dozens of monkeys all clamoring for attention. Fear is an especially loud monkey, sounding the alarm incessantly, pointing out all the things we should be wary of and everything that could go wrong".

It really is the mind that mixes us up the most. We need to ignore it because we are all just the way we are supposed to be and have all the talents and gifts to do whatever it is we dream of doing and being. Sometimes our monkey mind can even paralyze us. I personally think this happens more these days from all the toxins in our environment, food, and technological gadgets that surround us and connect to us, along with the way we work sitting all day at computers, smartphones, and video games for the most part that adds more stress most of us don't even realize and recognize.

Depression, anxiety and stress are on the rise along with higher alcohol and sugar consumption.

This gets our hormones all out of sync and decreases wellness and the chaos of our thoughts. Stress is the worst! The endorphin rush of physical exercise quiets the monkey mind. Therefore, even the youngest of us these days need to get out and do and watch the increased sugar intake in all processed foods even more today to maintain health and wellness. Unplug, get outside, go and do physical activity to adjust and condition mental health.

Sometimes the little voice stops us from being our true beautiful spirit selves. The people around us tell us things that make us feel bad and may not be the truth, but it hurts our feelings and makes us think we can't, are not as good as we really are or can be, especially if this happens too often when we are young and impressionable.

The simplest thoughts and comments crush our spirit most when we are young. Steve Harvey (2014) in his book, *Act Like a Success, Think Like a Success: Discovering Your Gift and The Way to Life's Riches,* related, "I was in sixth grade, and my teacher asked everyone in the class to write on a piece of paper what they wanted to be when they grew up. The teacher started calling our names and reading aloud what we wrote. I couldn't wait for her to call me. When she finally got to my name, she said, 'Little Stevie, stand up and come to the front of the room. … I just knew I had written something so deep and powerful … I want to be on TV. … She delivered her final blow when she said, 'Stevie, you can't be on TV. You take this paper home and write something more realistic and then bring it back tomorrow.'"

According to Dr. Alice Domar, clinical psychologist, contrary to popular opinion, talking to ourselves is not the first sign of madness. We all have a silent, internal conversation with ourselves, in our mind, almost all the time. This is called Internal Self-Talk and is totally natural and healthy. We have about 50,000 thoughts a day most of which are automatic. Our internal self-talk will be a mixture of positive, negative and neutral thoughts, (healthy self-talk ratio is around two positive thoughts to every one negative thought); it is important to understand that this internal dialogue can influence our feelings and behaviors. If our self-talk is mainly negative, harsh and unrealistic it can exacerbate any stress we are under. In this silent self-talk, we are often our own judge, jury and executioner with no right of appeal and no extenuating circumstances. We can call ourselves useless, worthless, stupid, a failure, horrible and this is a form of psychologically beating ourselves up, it is literally a form of psychological torture. Someone once wrote: 'If we talked to our friends in the same way that we talk to ourselves we would not have any friends.'

We tend to think our thoughts are just thoughts; they are not.

Research has found they affect brain chemistry. Quantum physicists state that our thoughts create our reality. Our inner voice, self-talk, is not fixed in stone. We need to be aware and alter our self-talk. If it is inaccurate and/or out of proportion it is important that we begin to change it. We can recognize and consciously change this self-talk so that it becomes positive most of the time instead of negative. We can change our inner voice to one that is more realistic, optimistic, and accurate. It is up to each one of us to do so, as it is a great way to improve our health and wellness!

When we begin to change our inner voice, self-talk dialogue as physicists have stated, so our thoughts create our reality, then we are speaking our personal truth and actively listening well to others without judgment to deepen understanding within our relationships. Authentic dialogue is different than conversation.

According to Merriam Webster dictionary, "Spoken conversation is the informal exchange of thoughts, information, ideas and opinions; interactive, communication between two or more people. The development of conversational skills and etiquette is an important part of socialization."

Some conversational related words are: "discussion, talk, chat, gossip, small talk." Some examples of conversation in a sentence are: "Do you remember our conversation about that new movie? We got into a long conversation about his behavior. The topic came up in conversation. They were so deep in conversation that they barely noticed me" (https://www.merriam-webster.com/dictionary/conversation).

Conversations tend *not* to be a back and forth exchange between two or more people who are mindfully present with each other, listening empathetically to all voices present, sharing and working in a sincere, safe, honest, and trustworthy environment together to produce or achieve.

"Shared meaning is the glue that holds people and organizations together. Good dialogue involves talking with our body, emotions, intellect, and spirit. Listening is a crucial element of effective, authentic dialogue. To have an authentic dialogue it is necessary for the participants to be in a mind-set of discovery" (Kohlrieser, 2012).

Research has shown that positive self-talk helps to reduce stress, and I for one try to work daily to reduce stress on myself. I work to consciously recognize my negative self-talk and cancel it and change it to a positive statement as often as I can that lessens the negative self-talk the more I stay aware and do it. I have learned to say no more often, not to overbook myself, and do what matters most to me – not everything. This is still sometimes difficult for me to do. I must tell myself to remember to slow down, plan, and prioritize my daily actions and not procrastinate. If I am procrastinating, I need to recognize I am just doing that and remember it is not serving me well. Is whatever that is causing my procrastination something I really don't want or need to do after all.

In the 21ˢᵗ century, when lives for us all are busy, we can all do more to limit our stress. Stress kills! It is not about putting a positive spin on something awful that happens to us, but it is about seeing the events that happen to us, in balance. The more we create a balanced lifestyle for our self and family, the healthier we will all be. This can be a start in the process – baby steps.

It is important that we begin to look at what we are saying mostly to ourselves. This is the first step towards changing our negative self-talk to become positive most the time. A good way to start is to write down the things we are saying to ourselves and begin to look at them for their accuracy. Then decide how to change those into things we want to say to ourselves and write those down to repeat daily, learn and try to remember them for the times the negatives pop up. Then we can cancel the negatives by repeating the positives we intend to bring into our reality.

Changing our self-talk doesn't happen overnight, because it has probably taken many years to attain the level of negative self-talk we have achieved, but thinking style is a habit and with time and practice we can change a habit. If we consciously work at it most habits can be changed in just three to four weeks. Then we just need to keep doing the *new* habit.

It is impossible and unrealistic to think positively 100% of the time, because a certain amount of negative self-talk can be useful to keep us safe, but it is about getting a healthy balance between the two that is best. More positive self-talk outnumbering the negative self-talk with neutral mixed in is the goal. Change is a work in progress with any habit we choose to change.

Changing One's Self-talk, Self-esteem, Self-confidence (Monkey Mind)

Davis (2009) explained, one's view of oneself derives from one's socialization. Childhood is a formative period of uncritical assimilation of cultural beliefs, socialization, and learning from significant interactive experiences with adult figures: parents, grandparents, teachers, and mentors. These experiences 'mirror the way [one's] culture and those individuals responsible for [one's] socialization happen to have defined the various situations'. Combined with other similar experiences, these meaning structures become our taken-for-granted frames of reference, habits, mindsets, points of view and ways of knowing and doing over time.

We rely on our cultural (socialized) frames of reference to diminish the chaos of our everyday world. These meaning-making structures support us by providing an explanation of the happenings in our daily lives, but at the same time, they reflect our cultural and psychological assumptions that have been socially constructed. These assumptions constrain us, making our view of the world subjective, often distorting our thoughts and perceptions. They are the double-edged swords whereby they give meaning (validation) to our experiences, but at the same time skew our reality.

We can learn to alter our habits, mindsets, points of view, and ways of knowing especially related to our inner dialogue, self-talk, internal conversation. We can recognize and consciously change this self-talk, so it becomes positive most of the time and much less negative. We each are the only one who can do it! Changing habits that may affect our health and wellness adversely is critical. Even though it may be hard work at first, just like properly feeding and hydrating our body, getting adequate sleep, and exercising regularly, it is best for us to work at trying to do it. It is each of our responsibility to do so for our self as each of us is the only one who can do it for our self; then we can do it for others: our children, our family, to teach, train and set the example for all those we love and serve. There are many ways to do this.

First, we have both positive and negative self-talk and focusing more on the positive cancels the negative thoughts immediately. When negative self-talk happens, consciously reframe it with a positive response throughout the day. Know that this will take time and is a process. We all need to continually practice cancelling the negative self-talk. Soon, our negative or fearful behaviors and feelings will become positive and less present.

The Buddha was the smartest psychologist I've ever read. More than 2,500 years ago he was teaching people about the human mind so that they might understand themselves better and discover that there was a way out of suffering. Buddha was a very wise teacher with keen insights into human nature. He learned much by meditating and learning from his own experiences, as well as by observing the behavior of others.

The Buddha and Buddhist teachings below present simple lessons we all can understand and practice to improve our awareness:

Buddha showed his students how to meditate to tame the drunken monkeys in their minds. It's useless to fight with the monkeys or to try to banish them from your mind because, as we all know, that which you resist persists. Instead, Buddha said, if you will spend some time each day in quiet meditation — simply calm your mind by focusing on your breathing or a simple mantra — you can, over time, tame the monkeys. They will grow more peaceful if you lovingly bring them into submission with a consistent practice of meditation. I've found that the Buddha is right. Meditation is a wonderful way to quiet the voices of fear, anxiety, worry, and other negative emotions. I've also found that engaging the monkeys in gentle conversation can sometimes calm them down. I'll give you an example: Fear seems to be an especially noisy monkey for people like me who own their own businesses. As the years go by, Fear Monkey shows up less often, but when he does, he's always very intense. I take a little time out to talk to him. For example:

"What's the worst that can happen?" I ask him.

"You'll go broke," Fear Monkey replies.

"OK, what will happen if I go broke?" I ask.

"You'll lose your home," the monkey answers.

"OK, will anybody die if I lose my home?"

"Hmmm, no, I guess not."

"Oh, well, it's just a house. I suppose there are other places to live, right?"

"Uh, yes, I guess so."

"OK then, can we live with it if we lose the house?"

"Yes, we can live with it," he concludes.

And that usually does it. By the end of the conversation, Fear Monkey is still there, but he's calmed down. And I can get back to work, running my business and living my life. Learning to manage your monkey mind is one of the best things you can do to transform fear. Pay attention to how your monkeys act — listen to them and get to know them, especially the Fear Monkey. Take time to practice simple meditation on a regular basis. Learn how to change the conversations in your head. Practice kind, loving, positive self-talk and see how it can transform your fears" (Gallagher, 2011).

When I was trying to finish my doctorate, and complete my dissertation, I had to spend almost all every day for four months on focused writing.

I had so much information in my head – the mind monkeys were driving me crazy! I found it hard to write about all I was trying to say to complete my scientific research discussion, results, findings, recommendations, and conclusions.

Early on in that process while having lunch with a long-time friend of mine and mentioning this problem to her, she asked me to join her meditation group on Monday nights. I remember thinking how do I fit that into my schedule. I shouldn't even take this time to have lunch even though she came to where I was to save time for us to eat together and visit. I needed to eat, drink, and sleep just to be able to keep going and process all well from the day before. Jo said, "Think about it. You'd love it!" I told her I would; I prayed and thought about it.

The meditation group met at her pastor's house; his wife led it. It was at 6:30 p.m. and with no traffic about a half hour drive for me. I had just returned from living, working, and doing research in mainland China and Hong Kong for the past five years. I didn't have a home of my own yet, as I moved back to San Diego, California instead of the cold in Eastern Washington State where I had lived and worked prior to going to China.

Life had happened over the course of those five years abroad, and I knew upon coming home that I wanted to be close to my children and new grandchildren. Before leaving Hong Kong, I asked my youngest brother, Ned, if I could live with him to complete my dissertation. He kindly agreed, and I am forever grateful. I was lucky he was a single, an entrepreneur, who owned and worked out of his home with room for me. What a blessing! I prayed long and hard about taking a break to meditate with Jo's group on Mondays. But I had to do something to change the way I was doing things presently to move forward. It was the best invitation and decision I could've made.

The group practiced, *Centering Prayer,* which is a method based on both the works of Ken Wilbur and Father Keating. Ken Wilbur "is a preeminent scholar of the Integral stage of human development. He is an internationally acknowledged leader, founder of Integral Institute, and co-founder of Integral Life. Ken is the originator of arguably the first truly comprehensive or integrative world philosophy, aptly named 'Integral Theory'" (https://integrallife.com/centering-prayer-origins-practice-and-contributions-integral-spirituality/).

Ken is a transpersonal psychologist, whose goal is to enhance the early works of Jung, James, and Maslow, the study of mind-body relations, consciousness, and spirituality. Transpersonal psychology is the study of human growth and development from a perspective that delves deeper into the inner soul. It has been defined as *spiritual psychology,* as "development beyond conventional, personal or individual levels."

Father Keating became aware of the Church's history and of the writings of Christian mystics during his freshman year at Yale University in 1940, which began his interest in contemplative prayer. He transferred to Fordham University's accelerated program while waiting to be drafted in WWII he received deferment to enter seminary. After graduation in 1944, he entered the Trappist Order monastic community at St. Joseph's Abbey in Valley Falls, Rhode Island at the age of 20.

"While abbot of St Joseph's, he invited Eastern meditation teachers to instruct Christian monks in meditation. As the Eastern teachers presented their practices, Fr. Keating realized that Christianity was largely lacking such injunctions to help cultivate a direct relationship with God. His longing for contemplative practices as a means to experience communion with the Divine Presence inspired the revival of Contemplative Christianity and the creation of the practice of Centering Prayer" (https://integrallife.com/centering-prayer-origins-practice-and-contributions-integral-spirituality/).

Centering prayer, like meditation, suggests one practice it twice a day for 20 minutes first thing in the morning and last thing at night to clear one's mind and center on the divine spirit within us all – love. You choose a word of meaning or image in nature, whatever that may be that is peaceful for you, sit quietly with eyes closed, and concentrate on your breath.

If thoughts come, and they will, simply repeat your word of meaning or see your image of peace to bring yourself back to a relaxed, centered state focused on your breath and freeing your thoughts. Your thoughts will come more often at first, and it is a process of practice that when continued over time calms them often. I was amazed at how even from the beginning this helped me immensely to be able to focus and write more profusely.

I also met new friends. I enjoyed the respite in the early evening and change of scenery from the rest of my week spent inside, mostly in my pajamas, writing. I realized how much more I achieved when I practiced meditation twice a day for 20 minutes. Some of those ladies have become life-long friends I stay in contact with today. The group membership over time has changed and new people come in and others go, as happens. Others are steadfast.

Linda, a wonderful friend, answered my prayer request immediately one evening after I had attended for several months and shared along with everyone else needs for others and myself. I shared I needed a larger space to leave and hang up my papers to look at for days to get all my collected data analysis done.

Linda had three children, all of whom had gotten their PhDs, so she understood my dilemma. Linda offered to let me stay in her home while she and her husband were abroad for over a month to complete the data analysis prior to getting further along with the dissertation write-up and completion.

She only asked that I water her rose garden, which I thoroughly enjoyed. She had a large home with a lovely guest room and bath, left their Internet for me to use, and there was a hot tub and pool in her complex. She even gave me their garage door opener so I could simply drive into the garage in the evening if need be and go right into their home. It was so lovely and such a gift and answer to prayer. I shall never forget their kindness and still consider them dear friends.

I took another dear friend from our Centering Prayer group, Sandra, to mainland China some years later as a teacher. It was an English Immersion Summer Camp Experience co-teaching with Chinese teachers, elementary and middle school Chinese students. I taught one high school class. Sandra agreed to go and recommended a few teachers to go with the others I had recruited.

It was my colleague and longtime friend, Beth's, company, InterLangua, for which I worked as vice president. We took teachers to China for three years to do this summer camp. It was such a positive, cultural experience for all from both countries; students and teachers learned a great deal. It was a huge success and resulted in Beth and several teachers staying to open an international school and continue that work there. I returned after that third summer and having another opportunity to travel more in China to continue to grow my own business, High Level Wellness with Dr. Ann.

I continue the practice of meditation still twice a day. I don't make it to the group much anymore, as I have moved residences and am not close. However, when I do have the chance to join them or go to a special event nearby, I do. Continual meditation practice still works well for me though. One can do it anywhere and anytime even for very short periods like waiting in an airport or anywhere you have some extra time.

Simply concentrate on your breathing and relax. There are many other practices like Tai Chi that is an aerobic, moving meditation and all kinds of yoga. Both add positive mental and emotional health benefits. Some schools and organizations are adding meditation to physical education programs with very young children to have them learn how to cope with their feelings better and behave well. Corporate leaders are incorporating the practice also to reduce stress.

Affirmation statements that you recite to yourself aloud excitedly also work to re-program your monkey mind to bring your positive self-talk more to fruition. We cannot let those rascal monkeys win. You can print out affirmation statements that resonate with you and post them in your bathroom to recite until you know them well enough that they become learned by rote. Writing out your intention(s), a plan of action to accomplish it/them, and a realistic date or dates to achieve a goal or goals works to bring it/them into reality.

There are so many things we all can do! One step at a time, consistently, act each day to move toward our dreams and accomplish them one at a time – you're a WINNER. Get going – don't ever quit!

Chapter Six

_____

Unearthing Your Power

We all possess more power than we can even ever imagine. Once we work toward not listening to those drunken monkeys. Accept that it is up to each of us to create the dream life we want to have. Being who "we each are truly meant to be" is a life process! There is no one else just like you or me. We are all life-long learners. Unconditional self-acceptance of who we truly are is key.

Let me define, then clarify the difference between self-esteem and self-acceptance. In sociology and psychology, self-esteem reflects a person's overall subjective (biased) emotional evaluation of his or her own worth. It is a judgment of oneself as well as an attitude toward the self. Shepard (1979) noted, self-acceptance is an individual's satisfaction or happiness with oneself, and is thought to be necessary for good mental health. Self-acceptance involves self-understanding, a realistic, albeit subjective (personal), awareness of one's strengths and weaknesses.

A more logical, realistic, and beneficial approach to the individual is an unconditional acceptance of the core Self, declared Shepherd (2017); the essential worth of an individual is unarguable, but the personality, the adaptive ego, may carry along maladaptive behaviors like tin cans trailing behind it.

"The individual and his/her learned and practiced behavior patterns or beliefs, are not the same thing. Every person is fallible and prone to make mistakes, indeed that is the only way to learn from experience, and every person is trying to achieve goals in life, whilst surrounded by all the difficulties and struggles that survival necessarily entails. To accept this about oneself is then to be immune to demands upon others' approval, and gives a greater freedom to act in a way that has reason to be right, rather than because a way is approved of by others. Unconditional self-acceptance is therefore a more realistic and aware form of self-regard, than self-esteem based on peer approval. And this awareness brings with it the corollary: an unconditional acceptance of the essence of others, friend or foe alike. To consider the essence of a person as 'unacceptable' is to insist that somebody should or must be different from the way they are and that is essentially irrational" (Shepherd, 2017).

For each of us to be able to unearth our God given power, we must possess total self-acceptance, meaning love, accept, trust, and completely know ourselves – who we truly are. Who are you? What are your talents, gifts and strengths? What did you dream about growing up? Who were your examples? As God's children, we are all unconditionally loved and accepted.

When I was growing up from birth to six years old, I had wonderful men and women in my family life as role models, prime examples, homemakers, healers, and peacemakers. As I spoke of earlier in this book, my NanaLou, Grammie and Grandpa, parents, were the influential people in my life.

They were influential not only by what they did but also while I was spending time in my home and their homes listening to them as they visited among themselves and with others. I learned and picked up so many things that I have been a part of and done related to those exposures. I have also tried to pass those down to my sons and daughter, son and daughters-in-law, and grandsons and granddaugh-ters whenever I have had the opportunity.

Today, in this our global 21st century, it is more difficult as many families are broken, separated geographically, and many children are not as for-tunate as I was to have family members very close for those first early years to pass on and nurture the self-acceptance we all need to gain when young to keep us rooted well and secure our self-acceptance.

This allows us to hang onto our self-accep-tance, as life progresses and its situations, episodes, and relationships challenge our self-esteem, but they don't rock our self-acceptance and regard too greatly.

Even though I moved often with my family when I was still very young until we stayed in Cal-ifornia, I instinctively knew who I really was when life's situations, episodes, and peer relationships challenged my self-esteem and I felt hurt and dis-respected. Those challenges were all lessons and teaching moments for me to overcome and remem-ber who I truly was what I wanted to be and do in my life. What was most important to me to achieve and become to serve, teach and leave to others.

My mother was a stay-at-home mom, great homemaker, and teacher whom I learned volumes from about being a lady and raising a family. When I was growing up in San Diego, most of my friends' mothers stayed home and didn't have to work. By the time I married, that was changing and has continued to be the norm since before the end of the 20th century for many households including my own. I was a single mother for years.

Today in the U.S. family compositions for many are different. However, I believe parents, grandparents, single fathers and mothers, aunts and uncles, other extended family members, dear friends, and mentors are still the role models, prime examples, guides, teachers, and mentors that hand down those lessons generation to generation to their sons and daughters. Prime examples that boys and girls learn to know where and how they fit within the dynamic of interpersonal relationships, what is important to them, their roles in society, how to create a successful, productive, and fulfilling life. This helps them to be less confused and conflicted about the peer pressure s/he faces.

We all know who we are – we accept our true selves completely. Our self-regard and acceptance is shaken by peer pressure from others, especially as we are challenged as older children (7 to 12), teenagers, and young adults.

Peer pressure attacks our self-esteem – our unfair emotional evaluation of our own worth; it is a judgment of oneself as well as an attitude toward the self. However, it is slanted and unrealistic. Our individual personal satisfaction or happiness with oneself, and awareness of our strengths and weaknesses, is our self-acceptance. Self-acceptance and self-regard involves self-understanding that is realistic, fair, and necessary for good mental health. We are all special, unique powerful human beings.

Today's women along with all the generations of our women ancestors and sisters of the heart before us are the peacemakers and healers of our families and relationships. The process of accepting who we are as women and stepping into one's unconditional self-acceptance is a learning process that we are challenged with daily. Loving ourselves enough to radiate our power, self-regard and speak our truth in love to empower our relationships with family members and friends brings moments of life-long learning and new discovery to each person.

Tony Robbins declared, "Regardless of gender, we all contain both masculine and feminine energy. Your leading energy reflects your inner nature and values. Because of this, there are men who have feminine leading energy just as there are women who have masculine leading energy. Understanding your leading energy, or core energy, is necessary to align yourself – or else you will be unhappy no matter how much you succeed. The feminine energy is always feeling and seeing everything. While the masculine is focused on one singular task or issue at hand, the feminine is constantly multi-tasking and processing everything at once. The right and left pars of the brain are active always. And there is an extreme power in this. When the feminine energy sees, or encounters a problem, there is a deep desire to share and connect. The feminine energy is nurturing, understanding, and all about intuition and feeling, while the masculine is about doing, the feminine is about being. The feminine energy wants to be sought after, pursued, cherished, and honored. The feminine energy wants to be wanted. What makes a relationship work is having things in common? But what makes a relationship passionate is having things that are different – not different values, but different energies. This is what creates sparks in the relationship. This is where the electricity comes from. So, if you are feminine in your core, then you will find commonality with another feminine energy, but you will find passion with masculine energy.

"When most people are stressed or tired, they put on the mask of the opposite energy. Most women, for example, who are feminine at their core, will put on a masculine mask. It is a protection mechanism. But the moment this happens, there is no possibility for romance. And to make matters worse, if you are with a masculine energy, it will only make matters worse, causing friction and disconnection.

"There are three triggers to watch out for that will cause a feminine energy to adopt a masculine mask: feeling unsafe, feeling unseen, or not feeling understood:

1. Feminine energy needs to be seen. It needs to know it is being felt and given attention to. Feeling unseen is the chemistry for a breakdown of the relationship. A woman who is feminine in her core, for example, and who

is not feeling seen in her relationship, will eventually seek that elsewhere.

2. The feminine energy also needs to feel understood. It doesn't have to make sense to anyone else, but empathy and compassion allow for a sense that there is an appreciation for what she (or he) is going through. A woman who is feminine in her core will not be able to let go of something until she feels understood.

3. Lastly, the feminine energy needs to feel safe. This comes from thousands of years of evolution. The feminine energy is the prey, and needs to feel protected.

These three factors are the life and death of a relationship with a feminine energy" (Robbins, 2017).

The most important of all relationships is your relationship with yourself. Finding your voice in relationships is speaking your truth in love always in your closest relationships the most. That empowering voice inside you lets you know just what that is and it is voicing the things you shy away from most often that you must address.

You know that is true to be true to yourself. Just as I do, you know it is the key! Take that leap of faith; unearth your feminine energies. Address that area and you will unlock all the areas of your life where you wish to move forward.

Unearthing your power comes from learning what lights you up from the inside. For women, this may be hard as we take on numerous roles in our lives – career woman, wife, mother, caregiver, volunteer, etc.

Think back to an earlier time. What did you relish doing most? For me, it was dancing and singing and wanting to perform and to be a doctor whose specialty wasn't clear until much later due to other life choices interrupting the accomplishment of that goal until later. However, many of my life's choices have been pieces connected to the aspirations of my youth. There are still some yet to be fulfilled and this book is one more.

The voice is a powerful tool; truth is meant to be spoken in all your relationships, even with yourself. We know our truest thoughts, dreams and goals. We must voice them aloud if just to ourselves. As quantum physicists understand, our thoughts create our reality. The universe, your higher power, and/or God hears your thoughts spoken aloud in time and space, then knows I am here, I am worthy, and I am ready.

Know you are on a divine path; we are spiritual, powerful beings in a human body and although each of us has lessons to learn and things to overcome, we are capable of so much more than we know.

Here are some things you can try that will help unearth your power almost anywhere you are:

Speak affirmations that resonate for you aloud and with feeling.

Step out of your comfort zone. Take those leaps of faith!

Do something brave!

Exercise your voice sounds – Google these and pick one or two to try to find one you like.

When you are speaking your truth in love, doing what you love will require effort, but come together and seem to flow more easily as it is meant to be. When you are feeling insecure, anxious, or shy, remember your true authentic self – who you truly are!

Chapter Seven

_____

Spiritual Wholeness

"Spiritual beings do not sweat life's small stuff. They also know that most of what drives us crazy in life is small stuff. The only thing that isn't small stuff is the reason you're on earth in the first place: to find that portion of the world's lost heart that only you can ransom with your love and authentic gifts and then return it, so that all of us can experience Wholeness"

– Sarah Ban Breathnach

Becoming more in touch with unearthing your power, finding true self-acceptance, knowing who you truly are and you are worthy, and what you value and want awakens your authentic gifts and talents to share what others are waiting to receive. It's when you know what you're doing is what you were meant to do all along. It is what you do out of love from the heart and fulfills you in turn to do it.

It flows together more easily albeit with effort and you seem to have the energy and resources for it all to happen even if at the time, you don't know how it will.

When we give up I need, I should, I must and dare to – risk yet plan, work and do all to make our dreams a reality – they materialize. Believe in yourself enough to step out in faith, go for it with an attitude of gratitude. Scientific studies found developing an attitude of gratitude is one of the easiest ways to improve your happiness and satisfaction with life. It opens the door to more relationships, improves self-esteem and sleep, reduces depression, anxiety and stress, so developing a daily habit of thankfulness for all you have affects your mental, emotional and physical health, decreases aggression and enhances empathy and mental strength.

I learned this lesson in my early 30s from the father of my youngest son, Micah. We were involved in a car accident in the 80's on New Year's Eve day on our way to visit friends for the holiday. My truck at the time was getting a new engine. I had bought an older, used Datsun sedan until the truck was finished. It ran well but a few things were not great on it.

Traveling through the desert on a two-lane road, the hood flew up, blocking my view. I was driving but couldn't see the oncoming cars or the shoulder side of the road. I slowed way down to try to safely pull off the road to take care of the problem. Before I could do so, a Sunkist semi-truck loaded with lemons hit us from behind. It sounded like a freight train was coming right through the car. It pushed us about 100 yards or more down the road before we spun around and slid, facing the opposite direction down the length of the truck along its side, and came to a stop.

My daughter, just five and son three, were in the backseat sitting down; we were hit so hard the driver's seat I was sitting in was knocked loose from the frame. We were in the middle of the desert – where if any of us had been badly hurt we most likely would not have made it. I was upset because the truck driver never slowed down or applied his brakes. They thought I had been drinking and I had not been.

So, I got mad; Joe said to me – you need to thank God — we are all fine. I will never forget it! I was truly blessed I didn't lose a child that day, God and his angels were with us. It took me some time to create a habit of daily thankfulness. And since then, I say, "I am thankful, and give thanks" most every day for the many blessings I receive. Those are the words I use and I repeat them three times when I say them because they mean a great deal to me. When I was living and working in China, I noticed the Chinese people repeat small sayings three times.

I don't honestly know why or what the meaning is behind doing so but it seemed to mean more when done. Sometimes they would bow their head a bit and put their hands together like a prayer. I liked it and adopted it as part of my habit when giving thanks. Having an attitude of gratitude is advantageous to our health and wellness; it has a myriad of benefits for us all. Just google it and see.

Spiritual wholeness is a state of robust good health and involves an attitude of gratitude, I believe. Robust is the opposite of weak. An attitude of gratitude increases mental strength along with physical and emotional health. It improves resilience to cope with trauma and enhances most healthy attributes.

Spiritual wholeness encompasses our holistic being – mind, body, soul, and spirit. "Whole" is defined, according to *The Free Dictionary,* as an entity or system made up of interrelated parts. Containing all components; complete not divided or disjoined, not wounded, injured or impaired. It is sound or unhurt.

Throughout the years, I have studied health and wellness, I continue to learn the truth of this definition. The wholeness of our body and its inner working, wonderful interrelated functional systems, are miraculous. Nothing mankind creates can compare. Health is enhanced through the feeding, care, and balance of those systems. Gratitude, along with good sleep (six and a half to eight hours recommended), getting enough water to keep our body's cells hydrated (at least half your weight in ounces per day), exercise (a body in motion stays in motion – at least a 30-minute walk six days a week), healthy food choices 80% of the time (nobody is perfect and we must celebrate 20% to do well the other 80%), and the highest quality supplementation (our body doesn't make all we need or get it from our foods today). If we work to keep ourselves at our optimum level of wellness instead of waiting until something hurts to try to fix it, we will have much less pain and suffering and a better quality of life.

The diseases we have today are lifestyle diseases. It is possible to ease those if we consciously choose to do so – it is up to everyone to choose.

I wanted to be a movie star and doctor when I was in middle school and high school. I loved Hollywood and so many of the old movies and worked at Circle Arts Theater in the round in San Diego as a teenager. Hollywood stars from Los Angeles came down to perform in its many plays and concerts held there. It fascinated me, and I loved to dance. I knew I always wanted to get married and have children, and the thought of traveling the world as much as possible to see all the historic places you read about, meet different peoples, and experience other cultures seemed so fascinating. One only must alleviate the Fear Monkey inside that tries to dismiss one's dreams from becoming reality.

If we create our reality by giving voice to our thoughts aloud, then our dreams are possible achievements. Positive, possibility thinking leads us to spiritual wholeness – the essence of who we truly are.

I didn't specify exactly all these intentions of mine or create a firm plan, step by step, with specific dates about what was to take place first, second and so on as to how all the pieces were going to come to fruition. In the process, life always happens. Events and situations over which you have no control take place. The best plans often are disrupted. However, most have and many more I hadn't thought out completely happened, as well.

All in all, looking back, the events of my life's experiences like puzzle pieces have fit together nicely while I was doing other things, learning lessons, growing up, changing for me to be ready as they came about. It is a process of becoming and each of us proceeds at our own pace.

I have had four children, three boys and a girl. They are all grown and I presently have nine grandchildren, five girls 18 to two years old and four boys 16 to four years old, that are the joys of my life!

I am so proud of all my children and grandchildren. I have learned and am still learning from them all. They are terrific people, teachers and friends, who I hope would say the same about me at this point in their lives. They are all living life, healthy and well, and seem happy, for which I am very thankful and blessed. We seem to have good relationships, and I see my children these days often. Three of them currently live in SoCal and hopefully the fourth will one day again too, so we will all be closer. Six of my nine grandchildren are now in SoCal too, so maybe the others will continue to visit and I will visit them too.

I hope to continue to get to know them all better, God willing, and travel with each one of them now that they are getting older. That is a dream I hope to bring to fulfillment. They are all God's gifts. It is our job to give them roots and wings.

I am thankful to have been able to travel abroad with all my children and create those lifetime memories that we all still cherish and seem to relive around the holidays when together. They have continued to take the opportunity to travel abroad as adults, I believe, because of doing so when young. It is one of the best of educational opportunities, as it shows an integrated history, other peoples and cultures, and our own culture and is an excellent lens through which to look at the world upon which we live.

I have met many dear friends and colleagues through my travels and life experiences. I have been blessed to visit here at home and some abroad, too, and cherish staying in touch with others now that there is the Internet and so many ways to do so.

I hope and plan to travel more when possible to see some of the places I haven't yet seen like Australia and New Zealand, Italy, Greece, and Eastern Europe, and visit those I know who have moved around as well. Our world seems big, even though we are closer today via technology and transportation than we once were it still is the only world we must live on – it belongs to us all. Spiritually aren't we all connected?

Ian O'Neill in *The Overview Effect* wrote, "Could be the best example yet of being 'spaced out'? When in space, astronauts have repeatedly reported inexplicable euphoria, a 'cosmic connection' or an increased sensitivity to their place in the Universe. The experience sounds like the ultimate high, or the ultimate enlightening; without trying, astronauts can attain a similar mental state as meditating Buddhist monks. So, what is happening when the human body is in space? Does zero-gravity create new connections in the brain? Or is it a natural human response to the vastness of space and realizing just how small we are in comparison? Whatever the reason, it looks like even when astronauts are back on solid ground, they have changed profoundly…as these several declared:

On March 6, 1969, Rusty Schweikart experienced a feeling that the whole universe was profoundly connected. At the time, he felt a euphoric sensation. "When you go around the Earth in an hour and a half, you begin to recognize that your identity is with that whole thing. That makes a change... it comes through to you so powerfully that you're the sensing element for Man" – Russell 'Rusty' Schweikart.

Two years later, Apollo 14 astronaut Edgar Mitchell (joint record holder with Alan Shepard for longest-ever moon walk of nine hours and 17 minutes) reported experiencing an 'Overview Effect'. He said the sensation gave him a profound sense of connectedness, with a feeling of bliss and timelessness. He was overwhelmed by the experience. He became profoundly aware that each atom in the universe was connected in some way, and on seeing Earth from space he had an understanding that all the humans, animals, and systems were a part of the same thing, a synergistic whole. It was an interconnected euphoria.

Schweikart and Mitchell's experiences are not anomalies; many other astronauts since the 1970's have reported this Overview Effect. Andy Newberg, a neuroscientist/physician with experience in space medicine, hopes to find out whether this is an actual psychological phenomenon. Perhaps there is a medical reason for an actual change in an astronaut's brain function when in space. What's more, he's noticed a psychological change in the men and women who have come back from space.

"You can often tell when you're with someone who has flown in space, its palpable" – Andy Newberg. Newberg has scanned many brains to try to understand how humans reach this euphoric state on Earth. The religious communities, transcendental mediators and others around the world can experience similar states and have been the focus of interest to neuroscientists.

In some cases, meditation leads some people to view the whole cosmos as an interconnected quantum web, where consciousness is not separate, but a part of the universe. Now, Newberg hopes to monitor the brain of one of the first space tourists so a better grasp of the brain function of a human in zero-G can be understood.

Edgar Mitchell has said that his personal event has changed his life, revealing a universe that had remained hidden until he experienced the

Overview Effect on that Apollo 14 mission in 1971. Whether this effect is a physical change in the brain, or a deeper, yet to be discovered event, Newberg hopes to find some answers" (O'Neill, 2015).

The interconnected relationships of Earth's systems and all on it is spiritual wholeness.

Chapter Eight

_____

Space for Self and Others

You never know a line is crooked unless
you have a straight one to put next to it.
                                        – Socrates

My doctoral work stated, authentic dialogic communication builds a space for self and others to co-create meaning making together. "A willingness to change may be expanded by learning how to approach communication differently. We can shift our understanding of communication from simply transmitting messages, naming or referring to objects, to the process by which we collaboratively converse, what we are making together and the actions that result. The self is a process that arises out of social activity and relations; it is within the continual making of relationships and experiences in adulthood that the self evolves" (Pearce, W.B., 2006, as cited in Davis, 2009).

Within long term, successful living/work experiences and engagements between individuals, couples, teams, groups, global corporations/institutions, this new communicative, social environment is a conflicting and contrasting one. This transformative learning environment of relationships, difference, critical reflection, and awareness of self and others transforms one's ways of knowing and being in the world, one's self-view, mind-set, points of view, and worldview.

Collaboratively conversing is different and difficult for most to engage in with others, as it requires taking a risk, being vulnerable, and we are not taught how. Most think it is arguing; however, it is truthfully expressing your own beliefs and points of view to discuss those with others. Individuals, couples, teams, groups, corporations, institutions, and other organizations are fearful to do this because there may be repercussions. False Expectations Appearing Real (FEAR) stops them. It does take some learning to do so, as one needs to feel safe and be trusted, honest, mindfully present, listen empathically, authentic, share advantageously, and work together to achieve results and produce something new that benefits both/all involved.

It is approaching communication differently to raise awareness, knowledge of self and others, and promote and prepare people to engage in conversing collaboratively instead of just talking to transmit information, thoughts, opinions, messages, ideas, and name and refer to things like the weather. Communication, the co-constructed management of meaning making, can create growth and change may occur in relationships of all sorts between any two or more individuals in social episodes, situations, events, and environments.

Davis' Enriched Dialogue model rooted in communication has the potential to transform one's self-view and others' by looking at who we truly are and what we are making together in relationship with each other. It is positive, possible, and inclusive of all perspectives. It concentrates on making and doing and looks at communication [naming, making, and doing] holistically, not through it, to solve problems of everyday life episodes, situations, and events. It has the potential to make better social worlds.

Word [learned] culture and tacit-acquired [unconscious] culture are languages. Tacit-acquired culture is a language of the past, present, and the future that is part of culture and of ourselves as well. These differentiating aspects of consciousness: identities, relationships, and cultures are socially constructed. Looking at communication and transformation from a social construction paradigm, distinguishes them 'both by what it says about things and by the things about which it has something to say'. Both transformative learning and social construction look at the action of communication, what we are making together. The practical application addresses increasing knowledge and awareness about: identities, differences, relationships, communities, and cultures that relates to authentic dialogue engagement to create space for self and others (Davis, 2009).

To further exemplify, Anderson, et. al (2016), stated "engagement is the willingness of both parties to commit entirely to encounters, and it requires 'accessibility, presentness, and a willingness to interact. ... the broader concept of dialogue can be defined as, 'an orientation that value[s] sharing and mutual understanding between interactants'" (Taylor & Kent, 2014-387-88).

Anderson, et. al cited Pieczka (2011) summarized Wierzbicka's (2006) work that emphasized dialogue:

- is an ongoing process that occurs in separate episodes,

- is an activity that usually takes place between two groups,

- requires a difference in viewpoints,

- goes beyond exchanging ideas and knowing what the other thinks; both groups come to truly understand one another's views,

- uses open mindedness to find common ground, but doesn't require a complete resolution of all differences or fully achieving a common way of thinking,

- requires respectful attitudes,

- refrains from attacks, and

- is viewed as valuable and productive and may result in areas where groups find they can think similarly, leading to a possible change of thinking on some points.

Above all, "'dialogue requires an effort to make ourselves understood, as well as try to understand, and here, the 'right' attitudes, motivations, as so on, will not suffice" (Wierzbicka, 2006, p. 700). The willingness to change these meaning making structures or not is everyone's choice. Some may not be willing or desire to change.

I found when around those from different cultures, within the U.S. and traveling abroad, that those experiences caused me to see the difference in myself as much as the differences in another's culture. I noticed differences I hadn't thought about in my culture that weren't the same in others, like when I was 25 traveling in Mexico, so different from the Germanic language based English spoken in the U.S. My voice when spoken sounded to me like a pebble falling the wrong way on the spokes of a wheel compared to the romance language base of the Spanish language that rolled off their tongues.

Many differences I noticed in the U.S. were due to religious beliefs, holiday celebrations, and different geographical or cultural food preferences. Things that were innate to me because of my culture differed in other cultures, like what side of the stairs to go up or go down, words that differ from one English language to another, like in Britain they say, "knackered," and in the U.S., we say "tired."

Also, what signs meant and where they were placed for everyday needs, like toilets and exits or trying to take a siesta when once we finished kindergarten or preschool, only to be told no more naps.

Here are a few excerpts from researched multicultural interviews I did on the social construction of transformative learning that affected change:

Dr. Zhang, from mainland China, stated it's very hard to change and so something similar to that is exposures, different traveling experiences, educational and working, it opens me up and gives me more perspectives. So, when I go back to China where I grew up, even though they are different, we are co-related, we are overlapped because we are all human beings.

Edward, from England, testified on a personal level I became a lot more confident just having to deal with all sorts of different situations and ideas. I became much more confident as a person, but as a British person it was strange because I'd never considered myself to be British. But in going somewhere else, all of a sudden you become British. You have to; you're almost an ambassador of Britain. And so you become more British; then you start to realize things that maybe you do that you never even really noticed before that people pick up and you don't. You just think it's normal, and so you're exposed. You know people can see. So that was quite different.

I found several factors that most participants described aided their success and resulted from their willingness to change. Factors rooted in communication related to cultural difference, relationships, and transformation encompassed within the multicultural experiences of everyday life activities were:

• increased self-esteem	• accepting
• confidence	• creative
• belonging	• outspoken
• a sense of community	• suspension of judgment
• growth in positive ways	• easier ability to take risks
• becoming more open	• gained new perspectives; new skills were acquired
• respectful	

Table 2: Factors rooted in communication related to cultural difference, relationships, and transformation

Toward an Inclusive Space for Self and Other

One's self-view is formed by one's culture. Culture characterizes the human species and also simultaneously differentiates one social group from another. Hall (1998) asserted communication underlies everything:

> Any culture is basically a system of creating, sending, storing and processing information, and cultural communication is deeper and more complex than spoken or written messages. Humans are guided by two forms of information assessed in two different ways: type A — manifest culture — which is <u>learned</u> from words and numbers, and type B — tacit-acquired [unconscious] culture — which is not verbal but is highly situational and operates according to the rules, which are not in awareness, not learned in the usual sense but acquired in the process of growing up or simply being in different environments. In humans, acquired culture is made up of hundreds and possibly thousands of micro-events comprising the corpus of the daily cycle of activity, the spaces we occupy, and

the way we relate to others, in other words, the bulk of experiences of everyday life. This tacit, the taken-for-granted aspect of culture, a natural part of life is the foundation on which rests 45 years of Hall's scholarly research (p. 54).

Type B — tacit-acquired culture corresponds with an integral understanding of transformative learning and coordinated management of meaning's theories primary question: what we are making together. It examines the transactions [communication experiences of everyday life] at cultural interfaces (spaces we occupy). The interfaces reveal the conflicting and contrasting patterns about both types of culture such as, the interviews of participants' successful long term living/work experiences in non-native cultures. Another way of illustrating interactions at cultural interfaces, what we are making together, is the figure/ground (participants and their environments and/or the disorienting dilemmas within intracultural/intercultural experiences) phenomenon that can be seen in the ambiguous drawing below, Kvale (1996) first introduced by Rubin, a Danish psychologist.

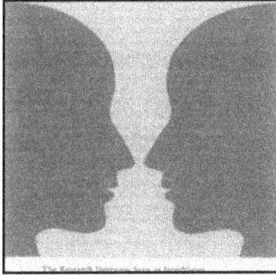

The Research Interview seen as InterViews:
a conversation between the two faces
on a white background or the InterView:
what is being made, co-constructed, the
between-ness, link, hyphen (the intersecting
white space shaped like a vase;
the self-other orientation).

Let me illustrate the phenomena yet another way using an InterView from my research: Dr. Penny Lau, from China, expressed these feelings that "I am a much more open and outspoken person than I ever was. I still hold onto my values, but I also feel everyone is allowed to make new choices and deserves a good life. The strongest, conflicting transformation that I have experienced and have difficulties with still is from my kids. When I went to the U.S., I was almost 30, so I had already formed a clear set of values and standards. They were exposed to a very different set of U.S. values. Being a parent in Chinese culture, we believed that children should listen to you. We believed for kids all we need to do is provide the best we can that was the Chinese traditional way before the one child policy now. It is different from the American way. Now, my son is 17 and saying that we never communicate. We never talked, and it's shocking to me! But when I think back, it's true. It started when we came back to Hong Kong when he was 11 and in middle school. Between the teenage changes, cultural differences, and conflicts of instruction, I think he also had a tough time. Already now he is in college, but I'm still, I'm trying and barely starting to understand him, getting on, and talking with him, so that part is the biggest difficult frustration, to call it, because if I had stayed in China then I probably would not have had all these problems."

This space Dr. Lau mentions is the co-constructed dialogue-between-ness, the transformed interpersonal/intercultural communication frustration that she and her son had and continue to have as their communicating with each other evolves along with its continued transformative process.

Kumar, from India, puts it this way when re-counting his innumerable long-term experiences concerning cultural difference: "I was interested in my culture more when I lived abroad, like an eye-opener so rich, intuitive, and so much more intellectually satisfying to treasure my philosophy not in an exclusive way, but I could say I saw my-self the same and yet different. It changes you and your teaching experiences, so you learn to become more adaptable and flexible. It is another learning process; one negative is one doesn't feel at home anywhere, but now I am a world citizen."

Jarrett, from South Africa, responded to my query, "When I went back to South Africa, I was a different person. I had been in a relationship prior to going to the U.S.A., which was put on hold. Ob-viously when I came back from the States, I would pick up and continue. But I couldn't because I was a different person, and this relationship was no longer compatible with who I was. I had definitely changed. I think it was purely in terms of just say-ing I can do anything that I want to do; therefore, it kind of changed the way that I approached every-thing. I couldn't tell the difference, and it was only after, honestly, about 10 years that I realized how much I had changed in my overseas experiences. I think America definitely did that for me. I had an achieving outlook. If I wanted to do something, all I had to do was do it."

Mei Mei, from Hong Kong, told about who she had become when she expressed, "The experiences I had in Canada have encouraged me to be myself or to enjoy being whoever I am. It was a wonderful experience! Every time I think back to its environment, it's very supportive, very accepting. A lot less, a lot fewer regulations, rules to follow and stuff like that. It's a funny thing because I keep being asked by others, 'So what do you consider yourself to be? Are you a Chinese or are you a Canadian?' And nowadays I just answer, yes, well I'm Canadian-Chinese or Chinese-Canadian whichever I am able to be, Yes, I am both. Because I have to be fair to Canada, all the experiences I've had there. It's a country that helped me to grow up a lot in a very positive way. The whole country is more accepting whereas here it's a lot more judgmental, and we have to fit a certain form, we have to behave in a certain way. I consider myself a true East meets West type of creation."

The evolving of one's self-view toward an inclusive, worldview fosters the process of change. We seek to communicate our identities as part of who we are, and who we are is continually evolving due to our everyday interactions and experiences. These myriad communicative experiences transform our identity and how we label them (e.g. "now I am a world citizen, I'm Canadian-Chinese or Chinese-Canadian, whatever, I become more British, and I have so many perspectives, more complimented, more mixed, more overlapped").

The making anew of the opinions of oneself, consciousness, relationships, and difference lead to the common within us all.

If instances of communication are socially constructed, 'we can create a more life-affirming reality by attending to our communicative behavior and choosing communicative acts that are more likely to improve than worsen our life situations' (Galanes, 2006, p. 2 as cited in Davis, 2009).

This is the goal of many academic courses and organizational training programs and initiatives such as: interpersonal and intercultural communication, diversity courses, global studies, human development, integral studies, organizational training programs on safe space, discrimination, harassment, public relations and programs for leadership, organizational development, and organizational change.

Through increased awareness, open mindedness, looking at varied situations and episodes as examples for investigation, and with models to guide us, we can scrutinize all sides of a story or concept, so that all perspectives are given voice to re-solve issues and re-author stories, become equitable, to change beliefs, and/or result in learning for social justice.

One participant from Canada, Mary, who contributed her voice for my research study gave a simple image of how context and understanding might be misconstrued, misinterpreted, and/or misunderstood.

"I often overheard teachers talk a lot about students and the quality of students many of whom were immigrants and had just come from abroad. I had one of those students in my accounting class, I couldn't believe it, there was a problem about if you went to the store and bought 10 donuts and each donut cost $1 how much would you have to pay? He just looked at me, and I said, 'You don't understand what a donut is, right?' And he said, 'No, I don't know what a donut is.' Since I had just come home from Africa, I knew [donut was a foreign concept]. But when teachers here at home are talking about how dumb their students are, I just think maybe they don't really have the same experiences."

Just as when we visit other native English speaking countries like Australia, Belize, Canada, many Caribbean Islands, Ireland, Jamaica, New Zealand, and the United Kingdom, there are many cultural sayings and things that most from the U.S. might not understand. They might need to ask for clarification regarding the meanings.

If we don't make assumptions but ask questions, for clarification, and further explanation without judgment and/or diminishing one's ability or know-how, it may further learning and understanding of alternative perspectives and lead to change.

There is no such thing as getting too much information and asking too many questions, especially when communicating within and/or between cultures and where learning is concerned. You need to exhaust all possibilities.

Sometimes the questions we might ask are not even known at first, so double checking and asking in a variety of ways is a good idea. Miscommunication happens time and again when we are speaking the same language, let alone communicating between cultures even with those in our own country. It also may enable both and/or all people involved in the clarification process to learn and discover something new from it.

It is in the InterView, between-ness connection that the *extra*-ordinary is formed and where conjoint, co-created, co-related creativity resides. Where the bridges and changes are built, the blends occur that produce discovery – new-ness that we wonder and marvel at, like mixing red and yellow to make orange, yellow and blue to make green, or blue and red to make purple, to say nothing of how far this 'making' of different hues can go and what might be accomplished if we act on that making.

We can make and relish in so many hues. The global citizen of today is a blending of many hues. Today's global citizen is a person who is socially and psychologically a product of the interweaving of social and cultural relationships, traveling, working, and living experiences and an innovation of our transportation and technological revolution. With the overlaps within our global village, are we not challenged to take a radically different approach to communication to make better social worlds and become global citizens?

In taking the communication perspective toward treating such things: beliefs, personalities, attitudes, power relationships, and social and economic structures as made, not found, they are seen as constituted in patterns of communicative action. We can then look at what makes a good communication process to bring about changes in our reciprocated communicative behavior and acts.

Communication is an observable practice of a relationship (Pearce, 2007 as cited in Davis, 2009). This might then be applied across disciplines in academia and within organizations by examining the contexts of relationships. Processes, however, require participation and reciprocity along with work and a time commitment from everyone involved for growth and change. This way of thinking requires holding multiple ways of knowing, being open to conflict and contrast that spurs us onto imagine, innovate, create, experience possibilities in the link of between-ness.

Like the ambiguous drawing of the two faces, there are unknown, unheard, untold ways to make meaning that have yet to be discovered. Realizing everything that is known is a questionable form of objectivity, always subject to difference and transformation.

This approach to relational knowing is a "self-transforming self" consciousness; a consciousness process of glocal[1] meaning making that is rooted in who am I as an interdependent part of human life on this planet, but is also open to being a part of the evolving, pluralistic, postmodern global systems within which one's co-related glocal consciousness is a vital part and out of which a continually changing worldview is formed.

It is in one's realization that multiple self-views are possible that leads to truth and reality, and one's holding that truth and reality are just as real as having one self-view. This multiplicity or glocal consciousness of 21st century global citizens may change social worlds for the better, "expanding the

---

1   Glocal represents the blending of one's cultural self-view and others' cultural perspectives, a meaning making process that is rooted in who I am as an interdependent part of human life on this planet that one chooses from all possibilities as their self-other orientation in our pluralistic, postmodern society of the 21st century.

boundaries of transformative learning" and moving "learning toward an ecological consciousness".

Research and practice that promotes behavior,
patterns, and processes of reciprocated communicative action that transform not only self-views but
worldviews work toward promoting these goals.

Chapter Nine

————————————

Coming Full Circle

The journey of writing, *Finding Your Voice in Relationships,* has been my continual journey to find my voice in all my life's relationships, learn more about how to achieve this to enhance all areas of my life's relationships, and it will continue to be a process I work to improve with all others with whom I am blessed to connect and collaboratively converse.

This book discusses some of the memorable episodes, situations, and experiences that have helped me to know and accept "who I truly am" and to share those with my reading audience so that it may raise awareness and hopefully help others.

"Life is not somewhere waiting for you, it is happening in you. One day it just clicks… you realize what's important and what isn't. You learn to care less about what other people think of you and more about what you think of yourself. You realize how far you've come and you remember when you thought things were such a mess that you would never recover. And you SMILE! You smile because you are truly proud of yourself and the person you've fought to become" — Unknown.

"Breathe, my friend. You are not old, you are young. You are not a mess, you are normal. Extraordinary, perhaps. In the blink of an eye your life will change. And it will continue to change for decades to come. Enjoy it, embrace it... be grateful for the ride. You are not old, you are young. And faith will get you everywhere. Just you wait" (Larson).

References

Anderson, B. D., Swenson, R. & Gilkerson, N. D. (2016). Understanding dialogue and engagement through communication experts' use of interactive writing to build relationships. *International Journal of Communication 10(2016),* 4095-4118. Retrieved from http://ijoc.org.

Breathnach, S. B. (2017). Wholeness quotes. AZQuotes.com Retrieved from http://www. azquotes.com/quote/962413

Davis, A. (2009). Chapter 7: Socially constructing a transformed self-view and worldview. In Fisher-Yoshida, B., Geller, K. D., & Schapiro, S. A. (Eds.), *Innovations in Transformative Learning: Space, Culture & the Arts.* New York: Peter Lang.

Domar, A. (n.d.). Session 5: Stress management for health course – Stress and internal self-talk. Retrieved from http://stresscourse.tripod.com/ id32.html#

Gallager, B.J. (2011). The Blog – Buddha: How to tame your monkey mind. *Huffington Post. http://*

www.huffingtonpost.com/bj-gallagher/buddha-how-to-tame-your-m_b_945793.html

Geisel, T. (1988). *Oh, The Places You'll Go!.* Dr. Seuss Enterprises, Inc. Random House Children's Books Division, Random House Publishers, New York City, NY.

Harvey, S. (2014). *Act Like a Success, Think Life a Success: Discovering Your Gift and the Way to Life's Riches.* New York: HarperCollins Publishers.

Integral+Life. (2004). Centering prayer: Origins, practices and contributions to an integral spirituality. Retrieved from https://integrallife. com/centering-prayer-origins-practice-and-contributions-integral-spirituality/

Kohlrieser, G., Goldsworthy, S., & Coombe. D. (2012). *Care to Dare: Unleashing Astonishing Potential Through Secure Base Leadership.* Jossey-Bass: Wiley & Sons.

Larson, A. (2018). Breathe my friend. *Goodreads, Inc.* Retrieved from https://www.goodreads. com/author/quotes/5804333.Abby_Larson

NAACP Evers biography. Naacp.org. Archived from the original on October 4, 2013. Retrieved June 13, 2013. Retrieved from https://en.wikipedia.org/wiki/Medgar_Evers.

O'Neill, I. (May 22, 2008 updated Dec. 24, 2015). The human brain in space: Euphoria and the overview effect experienced by astronauts. Universe Today Space and Astrology News. Retrieved from https://www.universetoday.com/14455/the-human-brain-in-space-euphoria-and-the-overview-effect-experienced-by-astronauts/

Robbins, T. (2017). Your leading energy is feminine. Retrieved from https://core.tonyrobbins.com/gender-quotient/thank-you-result-88OF-797PN.html

Scotton, B. W. (1996). Introduction and definition of transpersonal psychiatry. In B. W. Scotton, A. B. Chinen, & J.R. Battista (Eds.) *Textbook of Transpersonal Psychiatry and Psychology*. New York: Basic Books.

Shepard, L. A. (1978). Self-Acceptance: The evaluative component of the self-concept construct. *American Educational Research Journal.16 (2)*:139. doi:10.2307/1162326.

Shepherd, P. (2017). *Transforming the mind: Self-esteem versus self-acceptance.* Trans4mind, Ltd. Retrieved from https://trans4mind.com/transformation/transform2.16.htm

Sterling, A. J. (2017). The women's weekend. *Sterling Institute of Relationship.* Retrieved from https://www.sterling-institute.com/sterling-institute-who-we-are.php

Tyndale. (1989). Luke 1:37. *Life Application Bible, King James Version.* Wheaton, IL: Tyndale House Publishers.

Unknown. (2015, September 22). Life is not somewhere waiting for you it is happening in you. Message posted to http://www.positivethoughtsandmore.com/2015/09/life-is-not-somewhere-waiting-for-you-it-is-happening-in-you.html

Welty, E. (1963, July 6). Where is the Voice Coming From? *The New Yorker Magazine. New York:* Condé Nast.

www.ingramcontent.com/pod-product-compliance
Lightning Source LLC
Chambersburg PA
CBHW052043090426
42739CB00010B/2031